Toe-Up!

Patterns and Worksheets to
Whip Your Sock Knitting
Into Shape

Chrissy Gardiner

SYDWILLOW PRESS
PORTLAND, OR

Toe-Up!
Patterns and Worksheets to Whip Your Sock Knitting Into Shape

First Edition

Sydwillow Press
P.O. Box 13607
Portland, OR 97213
www.sydwillowpress.com

Cover design and interior layout by Bruce Conway and Chrissy Gardiner
Pattern and technique photographs by Gail Marracci
Author and introduction photographs by Bill Gardiner and Janet Jennings
Technical editing by Amanda Woodruff and Amy Polcyn

Printed in Canada by Friesens

Mixed Sources
Cert no. SW-COC-001271
© 1996 FSC
FSC

ISBN: 978-0-9819668-0-9
Library of Congress Control Number: 2009902557

This book uses the Knitter's Symbol Font for all charts, courtesy of Aire River Design, http://home.earthlink.net/~ardesign/

For Bill,
who very rarely complains
about all the yarn.

Table of Contents

View from west side of San Juan Island, Washington, near Lime Kiln State Park, looking south towards the Olympic Peninsula. Much of this book took shape in this breathtakingly beautiful part of the world.

Acknowledgements

This book would not have happened without the support and dedication
of so many amazing people.

Thank you to my skilled (and fast!) sample knitters, Katrina Cunningham,
Kristie Naranjo, Zona Sherman and Lisa Hoaglund.
You saved my wrists and my sanity with your nimble fingers.

Thank you to my talented, tolerant photographer Gail Marracci for all the last-minute
photo sessions and endless afternoons searching for that perfect shot.
This book is what it is because of your passion for photographing knits.

Thank you to my invaluable team of test knitters: Lisa, Robin, Carol, Amanda,
Linda, Dustina, Alice, Beth, Julie, Michelle, Tina, Jennifer and Becky.
These patterns are infinitely more accurate and knittable thanks to your efforts.

Thank you to my amazingly dedicated technical editors, Amanda Woodruff
and Amy Polcyn. Your eagle eyes always keep me honest!

Thank you to my team of proofreaders: Ariel Altaras, Emily McKeon, Julie Ballinger,
and Michelle Tang. You caught my typos and grammatical irregularities as well as
contributing your fun little ideas to the finished book (thank you, Julie, for the footprints!).

Thank you to my book designer, Bruce Conway, who is able to see how things should fit on
the printed page in a way that escapes me. I don't always know what I'm looking for until
I see it, and you brought the book I wanted to see to these pages.

Thank you to Margaret Fisher and Janel Laidman, for paving the way with your own
beautiful books. You gave me the confidence to try this for myself.

Thank you to all the Visionaries from Cat Bordhi's annual Visionary Retreat for
Self-Publishing Authors on San Juan Island in Washington.
You've all helped me with this book more than you will ever know.

Thank you especially to Cat, for taking us all under your wing and helping us learn how to fly. I still wonder every day at my good fortune in finding myself under your tutelage.

Thank you to Judy Becker for inventing your wonderful cast-on and sharing it with the world so generously.

Thank you to Emily McKeon for your incredibly helpful edits and the Wednesday morning phone calls. You're up next, baby!

Thank you to Leslie Cumming for the long walks and chats over coffee. You're my one-woman cheerleading squad.

Thank you to Donna Arney for keeping Gardiner Yarn Works chugging along while this book sucked up most of my spring.

Thank you to my mother-in-law, Sue Gardiner, for always believing in me (and for all the babysitting!). You truly are a second mother to me.

Thank you to my mom, Janet Jennings, for keeping my commas in line and raising me to be a reader, writer and avid crafter.

Thank you to my tolerant, loving children, Sydney and Owen. I apologize that you never have any hand-knit socks of your own to wear. When this book is finished, I promise to make you some.

Thank you to my husband, Bill, for putting up with the knitting madness with gentle good-humor, as well as adeptly talking me down off the ledge whenever I need it. You are my #1 cheerleader and I adore you for it.

Finally, thank you to all of the knitters who have put your faith in me enough to knit something from one of my patterns. I so appreciate your trust. Thank you for all of your words of encouragement and gentle inquiries when those inevitable errata rear their ugly heads. You are all my partners in this knitterly endeavor, so keep up the good work!

Introduction

Welcome to the wonderful world of toe-up sock knitting. I must admit, I never thought I'd write a book on toe-up socks. I was truly a traditionalist, clinging stubbornly to my top-down technique. Fortunately, I don't like to admit that I can't master a particular technique, so I grudgingly taught myself to knit toe-up socks. I started with one pair and, frankly, didn't really enjoy it.

When I was asked to design a couple pairs of toe-up socks, I started to play around with different heels and toes. Then I started teaching sock classes at *Twisted*, my neighborhood yarn shop here in Portland.

We initially offered both top-down and toe-up introductory sock classes. The toe-up classes filled instantly while the top-down were considerably less popular. I resigned myself to teaching the toe-up method, wrote up my *Mix-and-Match Rib Toe-Up Sock* pattern leaflet, and slowly came to appreciate the benefits and charms of knitting my socks starting at the toe. These days, it's the way I find myself casting on for most of my socks.

If you're a veteran sock knitter, you can take a pick-and-choose approach to this book, focusing on the patterns that you *Must! Knit! Now!* while playing around with the techniques they include.

Just An Aside. You may want to briefly skim over the technique chapters before you get started to see if there's anything with which you aren't yet familiar, paying particular attention to the boxes (like this one) marked with the footprint icon that include important tips on how to use the patterns in this book, as well as some of my favorite sock-knitting tricks.

If you're new to socks, here's a warning: They are strangely addictive! I knit them everywhere I go.

Before I learned to knit them I couldn't quite understand why anyone would want hand-knit socks. My impression was that they were thick, uncomfortable, scratchy and impossibly old-fashioned. Was I wrong!

Sock knitting is a world unto itself with an endless array of yarn choices, pattern options and a surprising number of techniques. Who knew that there could be so many different ways to turn a heel?

I find the sock shape to be the perfect palette for playing with complicated stitches and color. It's much less of a time and yarn commitment than an adult-sized sweater, and I find that I'm willing to wear a much wider array of colors and crazy stitch patterns on my feet than I am on my back.

This book assumes that you have some basic knitting skills (mainly knitting, purling and an adventurous spirit). Check the glossary for unfamiliar abbreviations and techniques that are used throughout the book.

I've tried to use common terms for all but the most pattern-specific stitches, so if something doesn't make sense after reading through the technique description, try an internet search to see if there's a description elsewhere that clicks.

Most importantly, have fun with your socks! I truly hope that you come to love knitting them as much as I do.

 Just Google It! There is an incredible amount of knitting information available on the Internet, and I turn to my favorite search engine, google.com, to seek it out. I often encourage students in my classes to "Google it" in order to find alternate techniques or descriptions that might work better for them. Aside from the plethora of knitting blogs, many of which have detailed tutorials from recreational and professional knitters, you can find several sources for online knitting videos that demonstrate the techniques in action. The streaming video website, YouTube, has countless live-action video tutorials available. Simply perform a search using the name of the technique you are looking for. See the Resources section in the back of this book for a few of my favorite knitting-related and informational websites.

Chapter 1
Getting Started

Tools

There is some basic equipment you'll want to have on hand before you start your first pair of toe-up socks from this book. Pretty much every sock pattern in existence requires needles, a darning or yarn needle for weaving in ends, stitch markers, a measuring tape and a pair of scissors or other yarn-cutting device.

You may find that a small-gauge cable needle or set of short US0 double-pointed needles (dpns), a small-gauge crochet hook, and some locking stitch markers come in handy. It's also good to have a calculator in your notions bag, just in case.

Have On Hand... In order to avoid redundancy, you won't see darning needles or stitch markers listed in the materials lists of the patterns in this book - it's assumed you'll have these on hand, since you'll need them to make pretty much any sock from these patterns.

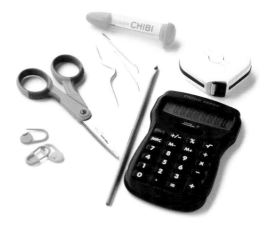

These are the tools I always have in my knitting bag when I'm making socks. You should be able to find these at your local yarn shop. You will notice that the yarn needles have a curved tip - this makes a huge difference when weaving in ends with the fine yarn used for socks. They come with their own little case, called a *Chibi*, and are manufactured by Clover.

At press time, the orange *Chibi* set came with three thin, curved-tip needles, perfect for use with sock yarn. *Chibis* come in several colors, each with different needle sizes and curved or straight tips, so be sure to check the package before you buy.

Needle Options

Obviously, you will need knitting needles to make socks. Although double-pointed needles (dpns) are probably the most familiar tool used for knitting socks, there are two other options that have recently gained popularity. Try all three of these techniques and see which you prefer.

My favorite method involves the use of two circular needles, but I have friends who swear by a single long circular needle (also known as the Magic Loop method) and know plenty of knitters who refuse to give up their dpns.

As with everything in knitting, pick the technique that works best for you. I have several sets of paired circulars and dpns in sock knitting sizes (US0 through US3) so I can grab whatever strikes my fancy as I start a new sock.

Choose Your Needles! The patterns in this book are written to accommodate all three of the methods outlined in this chapter. Each pattern gives a suggested needle size but does not specify type or needle length. Feel free to choose whichever needle type you prefer (two circulars, a single long circular or a set of four or five dpns). The patterns refer to "instep stitches" and "heel stitches" instead of numbering the needles. This allows you to divide the stitches according to the needles you're using without confusion. The instep stitches run up the top of the foot and front of the leg. The "heel stitches" include the bottom-of-foot stitches before the heel turn, the stitches used for the heel turn, and the back-of-leg stitches after the heel turn.

Double-Pointed Needles

If you are a dpn loyalist, it's easy enough to use your dpns for toe-up socks. You may find it a bit tricky to get started, since the needles aren't flexible and need to be right next to each other. Unlike a top-down sock where you start with an open circle, you begin toe-up socks at the closed toe and it can be difficult to manipulate the needles over the first few rounds.

If you find it really uncomfortable, try starting your sock on circulars, working a few rounds and then switching to dpns for the rest of the sock. There is no reason not to switch between needle types and use the technique that feels most comfortable for each sock section.

To knit your toe-up sock on dpns from the very start, begin by using your preferred cast-on method to make the correct number of stitches on each of two dpns. For instance, if your sock starts with ten stitches using Judy's Magic Cast-On, you will cast five stitches onto each of two dpns.

On the first round, divide the stitches on each needle over two dpns, so at the end of the round you have four needles with approximately $^1/_4$ of the stitches on each. In our example of ten stitches, you would work three stitches onto dpn #1, two stitches onto dpn #2, three stitches onto dpn #3 and two stitches onto dpn #4.

In this book, the instep stitches are worked first (with the exception of the *Fjordland* pattern) and in this case would rest on dpns #1 and #2. The heel stitches (those on the bottom of the foot and back of the leg) would rest on dpns #3 and #4.

If you prefer to knit your socks on three dpns instead of four, you will find it easiest to place the instep stitches on a single dpn and divide the heel stitches over the remaining two dpns. The stitches can be redistributed so that approximately $^1/_3$ of the stitches are on each needle once the heel turn is complete.

Personally, I find that this method puts too much pressure on the joins between the needles, but I know knitters who prefer it as there's one less needle to jockey.

Two Circular Needles

This is my favorite method for socks. I love how flexible the tube of the sock feels when half of its stitches are held on the needle cable. It also helps that it's not as easy for my small children to pull a circular needle out of a sock-in-progress - they can whip dpns out of my knitting with lightning speed.

You will need two circular needles of approximately equal length. I recommend 24", because shorter needles will put stress on the joins between the needles and may cause ladders (a column of loose stitches up the sides of your sock), and longer needles can get in your way.

You may find it helpful to mark one needle so that you know where your round starts. You can do this with nail polish, a stitch marker, a safety pin on the toe of your sock, or two different types or colors of needle.

The Amazing Addi Turbo!
In addition to having a favorite technique, I've got a favorite needle to go along with it. The Addi Turbo is made in Germany and has smooth nickel-plated tips connected by a flexible plastic cable. What makes it particularly effective for sock knitting is the butter-smooth join between the needle and the cable. Rough joins can be a real headache, making you pause to manhandle the stitches onto the needle tip from the cable. I've never had this issue with my Addis. Just be aware that the US sizes of the Addi needles are not always the same as the US sizes of other needle brands, so pay attention to the millimeter size, particularly if you're switching between needle types. I learned this the hard way!

When working in the round on two circular needles, half of your sock stitches will live on one needle and half on the other.

Using your preferred cast-on method, make the required number of stitches on each of the two circular needles. You will proceed to work around the stitches in a circle, making sure that the right side of the sock is always facing you.

The stitches on needle #1 will stay on needle #1 and should never be worked onto the other needle, and vice versa. If you accidentally knit some stitches onto the wrong needle, simply slip them back to the correct one.

To begin working in the round, slide the stitches on needle #2 (the heel/back-of-leg stitches) onto that needle's cable. Slide the stitches on needle #1 (the instep/front-of-leg stitches) onto the tip of the needle that is closest to the working yarn, making sure that the right side of the sock is facing you. Pick up the other end of needle #1 and use it to work across the stitches.

When all of the stitches on needle #1 have been worked, slide them onto that needle's cable. Slide the stitches on needle #2 onto the tip of the needle that is closest to the working yarn, making sure that the right side of the work is facing you.

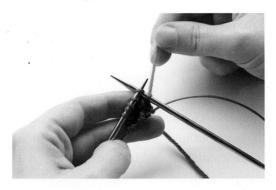

Pick up the other end of needle #2 and use it to work across the stitches. You have completed one round and can continue to the next round by going back to needle #1.

You can find complete details on this method, as well as a series of great patterns that use it, in the book *Socks Soar on Two Circular Needles* by Cat Bordhi.

One Long Circular

This technique was dubbed the Magic Loop method by Sarah Hauschka when she introduced it to us via the Fiber Trends booklet *The Magic Loop: Working Around On One Needle* by Bev Galeskas. Although she probably wasn't the first to work small-circumference tubes using this method, she gave it a memorable name and more than a little help becoming a common technique amongst sock (and sleeve, and mitten, and hat) knitters.

Magic Loop involves working around the circumference of the sock on a single long circular needle. The needle's cable sticks out of each side of the knitted tube, forming a pair of loops and providing the needed flexibility to knit in a circle.

Even though it is possible to use a shorter needle, I recommend starting with a cable length of at least 40". The longer cable will put less stress on the joins down the sides of the sock and will help prevent ladders from forming.

The concept behind this method is the same as knitting on two circulars, except instead of dangling needle tips, there will be a loop of needle cable at each side of the sock.

Using your preferred cast-on method, make the required number of stitches on each of the two needle tips, allowing the cable to bend in the middle and stick out to one side.

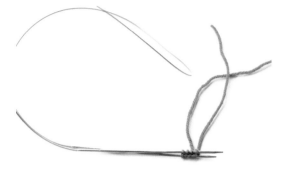

With the needle tips pointing to the right, pull the bottom/front needle tip (needle #2) through the live stitches so they rest on the cable of the needle, leaving a loop of cable sticking out to the left.

Bring the empty needle tip around, forming another loop of cable to the right, between the needle tip and the stitches on the cable. Use the empty needle tip to knit across the stitches on the top/back needle (needle #1).

When all of the stitches on needle #1 are worked, slide them onto the cable on the other side of the right-hand needle tip. Turn the work clockwise so that the needle tips are pointing to the right.

Slide the unworked stitches from the cable onto the empty needle tip closest to them (needle #2), leaving a loop of cable sticking out the other side.

Bring the other needle tip around, leaving another loop of cable between the needle tip and the stitches on the cable, and use it to knit across the stitches on needle #2.

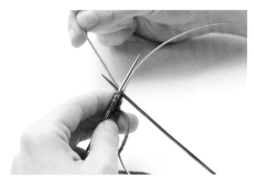

You have now completed one round and can continue knitting by sliding the stitches just worked onto the cable and sliding the rest onto the closest needle tip.

One Circular or Two?
Throughout this book, I refer to dpns or circulars. Although it may sound as if I'm excluding the single long circular method entirely, you can instead think of your long needle as two circulars that have a loop of cable in place of two dangling needle tips. The two needle tips of your long circular are the Magic Loop equivalent of two separate needles.

Gauge and Fabric for Socks

Socks need to be knit more firmly than other garments because they receive an incredible amount of abuse inside your shoes or, alternately, being shuffled along rough floors while subjected to your entire body weight concentrated on a small area of fabric.

To keep your socks from wearing out instantly, you will want to knit them on smaller needles and with a tighter gauge than you would use for a sweater or scarf. This will also prevent the uncomfortable tendency of looser stitches to imprint themselves into the bottom of your foot.

In my experience, the best gauge for socks is somewhere between eight and ten stitches per inch, depending on how thick the yarn is (thicker yarn will have fewer stitches per inch while still giving a nice firm fabric).

One great benefit of toe-up socks is that you can use your toe as a swatch. As you knit, you can try your little sock-in-progress on your foot at various stages and know pretty quickly whether or not it's going to be a good fit. If your stitch gauge is off when you get to the end of your toe, you can rip out without too much grief because, after all, it's just a toe.

I highly encourage you to keep a sock notebook in which you record your successes, including yarns used, needle size, gauge, and stitch counts of socks that fit your feet particularly well. You'll start to get a feel for what works, and this will allow you to confidently start knitting socks without a pattern once you get a few pairs under your belt. You'll also be able to invest in nice needles in a few of the small sizes (US0/2mm through US3/3.25mm) to cover pretty much any sock-knitting situation.

Remember that the needle size printed in any pattern is only a suggestion and you may or may not be able to "just start knitting" without checking your gauge. Once you develop your notebook, however, you'll be able to look at a pattern, see that it requires eight stitches per inch, and confidently select your yarn and needles.

Materials
Choosing the Best Yarn for Your Socks

Besides needles, yarn is the other critical component of your socks. In fact, it is probably the most critical, although the combination of yarn and needles must be appropriate for best results.

There has never been such an abundance of colors and types of yarn for knitting socks. You can choose cashmere, buffalo or alpaca fibers. You can opt for wool blended with bamboo, cotton or lyocel (commonly branded as Tencel). You can select from a rainbow of commercially-dyed solid and multi-colors, or find a one-of-a-kind skein of handpainted wool dyed with care in a yarnie's kitchen studio. You can make socks in thin fingering-weight yarn that knits at ten stitches to the inch or whip up a pair of worsted-weight boot socks that will wear like iron.

There is no limit to the fiber, color and texture options of sock yarn. However, there are a few things I've learned that, in my personal opinion, help socks and yarn play nicely together.

Color

Color is often the first thing that draws us to a skein of yarn. Who can resist the lovely skeins painted in a rainbow of rich colors? Hand-painted yarns are a joy to work with, but it's important to think about how the coloring of the yarn will work with the pattern of the sock you're planning to knit.

Generally, dark or highly-contrasting colors knit up best in simple designs. When in doubt, knit a swatch. You'll want to make a full-sized tube using the stitch pattern that will grace your sock because this will give you the best idea of how the colors will interplay with the stitch pattern.

With a hand-painted yarn, the length of the color repeats affect how the colors fall, and so a smaller swatch will look different than your finished sock. When I am designing with a particularly vibrant hand-painted yarn, it can take me several swatching

attempts before the yarn tells me what it wants to become. Hopefully you (or someone you love) will be wearing these socks for years to come, so a little up-front work is worth the effort to ensure they are spectacular.

If you've found a sock design with a stitch pattern you simply must show off, you'll get the best result with a smooth, light-colored yarn. Pale blue, green, gray, yellow, lavender and pink are all good colors to use with complex stitches.

Fiber

The vast majority of sock yarn is wool, because it is durable, warm and resistant to dampness. It's an unfortunate fact that the more durable the wool, the scratchier it feels (at least, that has been my experience).

However, there are a number of lovely sock yarns available that use softer wool and blend it with a small amount of nylon to make it more durable. Silk, bamboo and lyocel are also strong fibers that can add to the durability of your sock.

Another trait that makes wool good for knitting socks is its memory, or ability to spring back into shape after being stretched. Socks endure an incredible amount of stress while on your feet all day, so this springiness is a good thing. Yarns with a smaller proportion of wool may not have quite as much memory, meaning socks made with them may stretch out and lose their shape more easily. Alpaca is a wonderfully soft, warm fiber, but it has a tendency to stretch like crazy. Socks made from 100% alpaca could end up a few sizes bigger after they've been worn a couple of times. An alpaca/wool blend will help to mitigate this.

What if you can't wear wool? Fortunately, there are options. At press time, my personal wool-free favorites were Cascade *Fixation* (98.3% cotton, 1.7% elastic), Crystal Palace *Maizy* (82% corn fiber, 18% elastic) and Crystal Palace *Panda Cotton* (55% bamboo, 24% cotton and 21% elastic). Other non-wool sock yarns include SRK *On Your Toes Bamboo* (75% bamboo, 25% nylon), and Berroco *Comfort Sock* (50% nylon, 50% acrylic). Due to high demand, new wool-free sock yarns are being developed all the time.

Fit

Measuring Your Foot

To get a great fit, you'll want to measure your (or the sock recipient's) foot carefully. The most important measurement used in sock patterns is generally the circumference of the ball of the foot at the widest point (foot circumference).

When knitting a pattern with texture (knit/purl designs), ribbing, or lace, you'll want to choose a sock size that's 10-20% smaller than your actual measurement (or 10-20% negative ease). This will result in a sock that hugs your foot nicely and doesn't sag around your ankles.

When you get a few inches into the foot of your sock, try it on and see if you like how the pattern looks. You'll need to knit to the midpoint of your arch in order to really tell how it's fitting (incidentally, this is approximately where you'd start your gusset if knitting a hybrid heel).

For patterns that have less natural stretch to them (this would include twisted stitch patterns, cables or colorwork), you won't want to make the sock too much smaller than

your actual foot size or you may not be able to get the sock over your heel. In this situation, you'd want about 5-10% negative ease. Again, the best way to tell if your sock is going to fit is to try it on frequently as you knit.

Find Your Size. For the patterns included in this book, I've included only foot circumference measurements since foot length and cuff height are easily adjustable and so I've made them as generic as possible. In general, you can expect the following foot circumference measurements to correspond with the following "person" sizes:

4" = newborn
5" = toddler
6" = child
7" = teen/small woman
8" = medium woman
9" = large woman/small man
10" = medium man
11" = large man

Of course, you will want to take actual foot measurements to get the best possible fit. If you can't, here are some approximate foot lengths to get you in the ballpark:

newborn = $3^{1}/_{2}$"
toddler = 5"
child = $6^{1}/_{2}$" to 7"
teen/small woman = 7" to 8"
medium woman = 8" to $9^{1}/_{2}$"
large woman/small man = $9^{1}/_{2}$"
   to 11"
medium man = 11" to 12"
large man = 12"+

The second important measurement is foot length. To accurately measure this, stand on a ruler or tape measure with the back of your heel on the 0" mark and see where your longest toe lands. Since hand-knit socks aren't nearly as stretchy as commercially-produced socks (which generally have some type of elastic spun into the thread), they'll probably be longer than your store-bought socks.

You don't want to make your knitted socks too short, or the heel will pull down under the bottom of your foot. On the flip side, if you knit them too long, you'll end up with a bubble hanging off the back of your sock.

After you turn the heel, try the sock on. Stand up and walk around a bit. If it's not fitting correctly, take out the heel and add or subtract a few rounds to/from the foot. After you knit a few pairs, you'll have a good sense of where you should be starting your heel. Until then, it's a good idea to run a lifeline (see below) half an inch or so before starting your heel shaping. This will allow you to easily rip back without dropping any stitches.

A Lifeline is a Knitter's Best Friend! *Although lifelines are commonly described for use in lace knitting, they can come in handy when working on any project where you think you might need to rip something out to make a correction. To run a lifeline, cut a length of smooth, contrasting-colored waste yarn in a lighter weight than the yarn you're using for the sock (dental floss also works well). Thread it on a yarn needle and, starting at the beginning of a round, run it through all of the sock stitches, parallel to the needles. Leave the ends of the lifeline dangling. If you have to rip back, the lifeline will hold those stitches so that they can easily be placed back on the needles (you won't be able to rip back past the lifeline). When your piece is complete, grab one end of each lifeline and pull it right out.*

Fit and Function Versus Style

In my experience, there are sock knitters who want to knit functional socks that will wear well, without extra patterning or frills that may be uncomfortable in tight shoes. On the flip side, there are the knitters who seek out the most elaborate socks they can make and buy special shoes just to show them off.

If you want a sock that fits your foot like a glove and wears well in athletic or other close-fitting shoes, you won't want a sock with patterning on the heel flap or foot. Simple k2, p2 ribbing and a light fingering-weight yarn will result in a thin, comfortable sock that won't get baggy around your ankles.

For a super-smooth foot, don't start the ribbing until after you've turned the heel and are starting to knit the leg. Be sure to build in a little negative ease (for example, if your foot is 8" in circumference, calculate the number of stitches you'd need for a $7\frac{1}{2}$" or even 7" sock so that the knitted fabric will hug your foot firmly).

On the other hand, if you love the look of elaborately patterned socks, you may want to invest in shoes with an open back and a looser fit. I have several pairs of backless clogs and mules in a half size larger than I'd normally wear, which I use to show off my fancier knitted socks.

You should also be aware that more elaborate stitch patterns, such as that on the *Sakura* pattern in this book, may result in a sock that is less form-fitting and not at all utilitarian. These socks are meant to be worn like a pair of stiletto heels - they are for showing off (and you certainly wouldn't go jogging in them). Check out the *Fancy Socks* section of Chapter 7 if the idea of making art for your feet gets your blood pumping.

When gathering with a group of sock knitters, you will notice that shoes get kicked off as soon as people settle into their chairs. Nobody wants anything to interfere with the mutual sock admiration society!

Resizing Patterns

I've tried to include lots of different sizes for the patterns in this book, but you will notice that there are a few that only come in a single size. If you fall outside the "average" foot size, I apologize for this. The more complex stitch patterns are difficult to size up or down without significantly altering the look of the sock. However, I can tell you a few things you can do to make the majority of sock patterns fit you without a whole lot of trouble.

For a simply-patterned sock, you have a couple different options. You can add extra stitches (add the same number to both the instep and the heel for the easiest math) and recalculate your toe and heel based on the worksheets in Chapters 3 and 4. These extra stitches can be worked in rib or simply knitted, depending on how you think they will look with the rest of the design.

If you're willing to do a bit more math, it's possible to add a half or whole repeat of a stitch pattern depending on how many stitches are in the pattern and how much width you need to add to the sock. I find that drawing out the pattern on a piece of graph paper or in an Excel spreadsheet and then playing around with the placement of the extra stitches can help size up a sock quickly (or bring on the realization that perhaps this pattern would be better served by resizing without adding extra stitches).

If you'd rather not redo the math, or the sock has an extremely complex stitch pattern, you can still easily resize the sock to fit by working on different sized needles to change the circumference of the sock. It's likely that you will need to switch to a heavier yarn so that your fabric doesn't get too loose and flimsy.

Chapter 2
Cast-Ons

One of the biggest challenges posed by socks of all kinds (toe-up or top-down) is finding a way to smoothly close the tip of the toe. With a top-down sock, the toe is closed last, generally using Kitchener Stitch to graft the opening shut or by using the yarn tail to cinch up the last few stitches into a little donut.

When you begin at the toe, you need a technique that will give you a smooth start. There are plenty of options, starting with these three common toe-up cast-ons: Judy's Magic Cast-On, the backwards loop cast-on and the Turkish or Eastern cast-on.

I use Judy's Magic Cast-On almost exclusively, but I encourage you to play around with all three (and seek out others) to determine which one works best for you.

Judy's Magic Cast-On

We'll begin by discussing my all-time favorite toe-up cast-on. It's the one I now use in all my classes and patterns.

Judy Becker debuted her brilliant invention in the Spring 2006 issue of *Knitty* magazine (http://www.knitty.com). It immediately took the online knitting community by storm and has continued to spread like wildfire. To find Judy's expanded instructions, go to http://www.persistentillusion.com and click on Techniques.

Here's How:

Hold the needles horizontally in your right hand with the tips pointing to the left and drape the yarn over the top needle with the tail toward you and the working yarn (the yarn going to the ball) away from you.

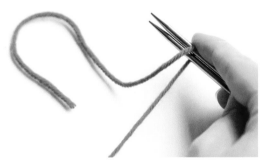

You will need a tail that is long enough to wrap around one needle *x* times, where *x* is equal to the number of stitches to be cast on to that needle, plus about six inches to weave in. Bring the tail between the two needles and to the back so that the tail is now away from you and the working yarn is toward you (the reverse of a long-tail cast-on).

The empty second needle should remain just below and parallel to the top needle. The loop on the top needle will be counted as the first stitch cast onto that needle.

Tent the yarn strands over the thumb and index finger of your left hand as if doing a long-tail cast-on. The tail will wrap around your index finger and the working yarn will rest on your thumb. Grab both strands of yarn with the remaining three fingers of your left hand and hold them against your palm in order to tension the yarn.

Stay Out of the Bermuda Triangle! When you're working Judy's Magic Cast-On, you'll notice that the yarn forms a triangle with your thumb as one corner, your index finger as another, and the needles as the third. When I'm teaching this technique in my classes, I tell my students that this is the Bermuda Triangle, and they should not fly their needles into it when they're starting to make a stitch. The needles should always go around the outside of each triangle leg to begin the stitch, and only briefly enter the triangle when capturing the yarn between the needles to complete the stitch.

Cast the first stitch onto the bottom needle by bringing both needles up and around the yarn tail on your index finger. It helps to anchor the first stitch on the top needle with the index finger of your right hand to keep it from slipping around.

The yarn will wrap underneath the empty bottom needle from back to front as for a yarn over. Slip the yarn tail between the needles to complete the first stitch cast onto the bottom needle.

There is now one stitch on each needle. Be sure to pull these first stitches firmly, but not overly tight. Pulling too hard will cause the bump where the yarn wraps around itself to pop to the front of the needles. If this happens, let the stitches relax a bit and gently push them back into place.

Cast the next stitch onto the top needle by bringing both needles down and underneath the working yarn on your thumb. The yarn will wrap over the top needle from back to front. Slip the working yarn between the needles to complete the stitch.

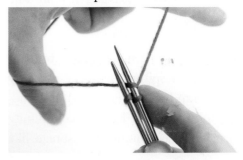

Repeat these last two movements, casting a stitch onto the bottom needle, then the top needle, until the correct number of stitches have been cast onto each needle.

Rotate the needles so that the yarn tail and working yarn are on your right. The working yarn should be coming off the bottom needle and the yarn tail off the top needle. Make sure the smooth side faces you and the bumpy purl ridge is in back.

You will begin the sock by knitting across the stitches on the top needle. Make sure to capture the yarn tail by placing it between the top needle and the working yarn before you knit the first stitch. You can gently tug the yarn tail to help firm up any looseness at the beginning of this round.

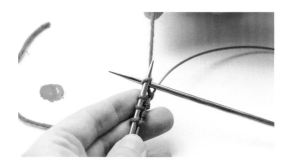

When knitting the stitches on the second needle during the second half of this first round, you will need to work them through their back loops to avoid twisting them.

You've completed one round and are now ready to start knitting your sock toe as written.

Turkish Cast-On

Another common toe-up cast-on is the Turkish or Eastern cast-on. It is similar to Judy's Magic Cast-On in that it provides a smooth, seamless start to your toe. It has a tendency to make looser stitches than Judy's and can require some manual tightening after the first couple of rounds. Give it a try and see which one you prefer.

Here's How:

Pick up a needle, make a slip-knot, and place it on the needle. Pick up a second needle and hold it together with the first in your left hand with tips pointing to the right. Put the needle with the slip knot on the bottom, with the working yarn coming up and behind the top needle.

Begin winding the yarn around both needles, coming to the front over the top needle and going to the back under the bottom needle, until there are the correct number of stitches on each needle (if you need six stitches on each needle or twelve stitches total, you'll wind the yarn around the needles six times). Do not count the slip knot as a stitch.

If you're working on circular needles, pull the bottom needle (the one with the slip knot) through so that the stitches are resting on its cable. The last loop should be wound around the bottom needle, with the working yarn ending up in position to knit the first stitch on the top needle.

Knit across the loops on the top needle. They will seem loose, but just go with it - it will turn out okay, I promise.

Pick up the working yarn and knit across the rest of the stitches.

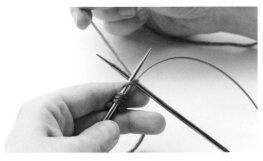

You've completed one round and are now ready to start knitting your sock toe as written.

Backwards Loop Cast-On

If working on circulars, pull the stitches you just knitted onto the cable of the top needle. Spin the needles so that the bottom needle is on top and pointing to the right, with the slip-knot in the "to be knit" position. Be sure to keep the right side of the work facing you.

Slide the slip knot off the needle, making sure not to drop any stitches from either needle. Pull the yarn tail to release the slip knot and move it firmly to your right (again, being careful not to lose any stitches).

If you find you just can't get into the swing of the other two cast-ons, give this one a try. It's also great for situations where you need a different number of stitches cast on to each needle, such as for the *Syncopated Rib Boot Socks*.

Instead of looping the yarn around both needles to get your toe closure, this cast-on starts with loops on a single needle and then picks up stitches along the bottom edge to complete the circle.

You will find that a crochet hook really comes in handy with this technique, so have a small one close by to save some time and frustration.

Here's How:

Pick up an empty needle and hold it in your right hand. Make a slip knot and place it on the needle.

With your left hand, stick your thumb up in the air like you are giving a "thumbs-up" sign. Grab the working yarn with your left fingers and hold it across your palm. Loop the yarn clockwise around your thumb so that the yarn coming from the needle crosses over the working yarn at the base of your thumb to make a circle around it.

Take the tip of the needle and bring it up alongside your thumb, under the yarn and inside of the yarn loop.

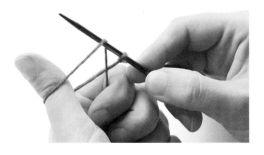

Slip the loop off your thumb and onto the needle. Pull the loop snug, but not too tight (or you will have trouble picking up stitches later).

Repeat until the correct number of stitches have been cast on, which in this case corresponds to the number needed for either instep or heel, or approximately half of the total number of stitches. Do not count the slip knot as a stitch.

Turn, and using a second needle, knit back across these stitches. Be sure to knit with the working yarn and not the tail.

When working the first row, do not knit the slip knot. Slip it off the needle and pull the yarn tail to get rid of the loop. This gives you a smooth, knot-free start to your toe.

You are now ready to pick up the remainder of the toe stitches across the bottom edge of the little strip you've created.

Hold the needle with the stitches in your left hand. Position the knitting so that it is on top of the needle, with the right side facing you, the cast-on edge pointing up, and the working yarn coming off to the right.

If using circulars, move the live stitches to the cable of the needle to provide a bit of slack. With a second needle, pick up the strand formed by the cast-on row above the right-most live stitch.

Wrap the working yarn around the needle as if to knit and pull it through to form a stitch on the second needle.

Repeat across the row until the correct number of stitches have been picked up and knitted. If you need a different number of stitches on one needle, you can pick up an extra stitch along this edge or skip picking up the final stitch.

When picking up the final stitch in the little knot-like bump at the end, the cast-on edge is often very tight. It helps to use a small crochet hook to pull up the last loop if you're having trouble getting it done with your needle tip.

You should now have the correct number of stitches on your needles. You're ready to begin working your toe in the round.

Chapter 3
Toe-Up Toes

Toes don't always get a lot of attention (at least, not the kind of toes knitted into socks). They're a critical component of the sock, but without the thrill of the heel turn or the glamour of the stitch pattern.

A notable exception to this toe neglect can be found in Nancy Bush's lovely book, *Knitting Vintage Socks*, which explores a number of different toes used in old sock patterns (unfortunately, they're all worked top-down).

I will not attempt to match her scholarly level of toe exploration here, but I will give you a few different toe options to explore when you're feeling adventurous (or if you find the toe used in a particular pattern doesn't fit as well as it could).

 *Worksheets! You will notice a series of example worksheets in Chapters 3 and 4. The numbers used in the example worksheets are from the **Mix-and-Match Rib Sock Recipe** and correspond to the Women's M (8") sock with 60 total stitches for the foot. In Chapter 8, you will*

find blank worksheets that you can photocopy to your heart's delight and fill out to carry in your knitting bag (but please don't share - if you find them useful, tell your friends to get their own book instead of hogging yours!). You can also download printable pdf files of abbreviated versions of each worksheet from w w w . t o e u p s o c k b o o k . c o m . You will need your book as a reference as you fill these out, but once you've got the numbers filled in, you will have everything you need to knit your toe or heel.

The Round Toe

The round toe is the workhorse of sock toes. It's the one that's most commonly used in both toe-up and top-down sock patterns. It starts with a flat edge at the tip of the toes, then increases smoothly to shape the toe pocket.

Non-Shaped Round Toe

The non-shaped round toe (as I call it in this book) increases at a steady rate, every other round, to form a little trapezoid.

This toe is used in: **Mix-and-Match Rib Sock Recipe, Gull Wing, Spring in Oregon** and **Sakura.**

❖ ❖ ❖

 Non-Shaped Round Toe Example Worksheet

Numbers Needed:

A <u>*8*</u> = half the number of stitches to cast on, generally about ¹/₈ of the total number of stitches needed for foot

B <u>*30*</u> = half the number of stitches needed for foot (this assumes that the foot has an equal number of instep and heel stitches - if not, see checks #1 and #2 in "Check That" section)

C <u>*22*</u> = number of stitches to increase on each half of sock, (B - A)

D <u>*11*</u> = number of increase rounds, (C ÷ 2)

Check That:

1. If B is not a whole number because the number of stitches needed for the foot is odd, round it down to the nearest whole number. When you are done with the toe increases, you'll be missing one stitch. Based on the number of instep and heel stitches needed for this pattern, determine where to add the extra stitch. On the last round of the toe, increase one stitch in the join between the instep and heel stitches and place it on the correct needle. You can also toss an increase into the top-of-foot pattern if it fits nicely with the design, assuming that the extra stitch is needed on the instep.

2. If B is a whole number, but the number of instep stitches does not equal the heel stitches, set B equal to whichever is smaller. An example of where this might happen is on a cabled sock where the cable pattern pulls in, requiring more instep stitches so it's not too tight across the top of the foot. When you are done with the toe increases, determine how many stitches still need to be added and to which side of the sock (instep or heel). Distribute them evenly around the final round of the toe.

3. (B - A) is a multiple of two. If it's not, increase or decrease A by one.

To Work:

Cast on (2 x A) <u>*16*</u> stitches, dividing them evenly across two circulars or four dpns.
Round 1: Knit.
Round 2: K-fb, knit to last two instep stitches, k-fb, k1; repeat across heel stitches. Four stitches increased.

Repeat Rounds 1-2 an additional (D - 1) <u>*10*</u> times. There are now (B x 2) <u>*60*</u> stitches on the needles (if needed, insert any additional increases in the next round). Knit one round even.

❖ ❖ ❖

Ideal Increases. You will notice that the patterns in this book use the k-fb increase (knit in front and back of the same stitch) for both toe and heel gusset increases. I like the way this particular increase looks with the second stitch (the increase) forming a small "purl" bump that lines up into nice columns when worked over several rounds and aligned properly. In order to get these columns to mirror each other on either side of the foot, you will notice that the k-fb is not worked in the same exact spot on both sides of the sock. This is because the increase forms a knit and a purl, and the purl bumps are mirrored by working the second increase a stitch earlier than the first. If you decide to work a different type of increase (such as a twisted yarn over or make one), you may need to move the spot where it is worked. You want to make sure that the increased stitch (the new stitch formed) is always worked in the space between the outer stitch and the stitch next to it.

Shaped Round Toe

If you have a wide, flat toe footprint (like the one I happen to share with Fred Flintstone), you may find that the non-shaped round toe doesn't form a wide enough pocket for your toes.

If you find that you have a little flap hanging off the tip of your toe, try substituting a shaped round toe. This toe increases every round for the first few rounds, then tapers off to every other round as it approaches the foot.

 This toe is used in: *Snuggalicious Slipper Socks* and *Vortex*.

❖ ❖ ❖

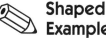 ## Shaped Round Toe Example Worksheet

Numbers Needed:

A __8__ = half the number of stitches to cast on, generally about ¹/₈ of the total number of stitches needed for foot

B __30__ = half the number of stitches needed for foot (this assumes that the foot has an equal number of instep and heel stitches - if not, see checks #1 and #2 in "Check That" section for non-shaped round toe)

C __22__ = number of stitches to increase on each half of sock, (B - A)

D __11__ = number of increase rounds, (C ÷ 2)

E __4__ = D ÷ 3, rounded to the nearest whole number

Check That:

All checks needed are the same as those for the non-shaped round toe.

To Work:

Cast on (2 x A) _16_ stitches, dividing them evenly across two circulars or four dpns.

Round 1: K-fb, knit to last two instep stitches, k-fb, k1; repeat across heel stitches. Four stitches increased.

Repeat Round 1 an additional (E - 1) _3_ times. There are now [(E x 4) + (A x 2)] _32_ stitches on the needles.

Next Round: Knit.

Next Round: K-fb, knit to last two instep stitches, k-fb, k1; repeat across heel stitches. Four stitches increased.

Repeat last two rounds an additional (D - E - 1) _6_ times. There are now (B x 2) _60_ stitches on the needles (if needed, insert any additional increases in the next round). Knit one round even.

❖ ❖ ❖

Anatomical Round Toe

If you're feeling particularly hard-to-fit, you may find it most comfortable to make an anatomical round toe which concentrates the shaping over your big toe and its neighbor instead of the center of your foot.

Instead of placing the increases evenly up both sides of the toe, they are instead divided approximately into thirds with ²/₃ on the outside slope of the toe and ¹/₃ on the inside. The result is a toe pocket that is pointiest above your two longest toes.

This shaping is mirrored on the other foot so that you have left and right socks, like your shoes.

 *This toe is used in: **Syncopated Rib Boot Socks** and **The Dude Abides**.*

❖ ❖ ❖

Anatomical Round Toe Example Worksheet

Numbers Needed:

A _8_ = half the number of stitches to cast on, generally about ¹/₈ of the total number of stitches needed for foot

B _30_ = half the number of stitches needed for foot (this assumes that the foot has an equal number of instep and heel stitches - if not, see checks #1 and #2 in "Check That" section for non-shaped round toe)

C _22_ = number of stitches to increase on each half of sock, (B - A)

D _15_ = number of outer edge increases, [(C ÷ 3) x 2], rounded to the nearest whole number

E _7_ = number of inner edge increases, (C - D)

Check That:

All checks needed are the same as those for the non-shaped round toe.

To Work:

Cast on (2 x A) __16__ stitches, dividing them evenly across two circulars or four dpns.

Round 1: K-fb, knit to last two instep stitches, k-fb, k1; repeat across heel stitches. Four stitches increased.

Repeat Round 1 an additional (E - 1) __6__ times. There are now [(E x 4) + (A x 2)] __44__ stitches on the needles.

Left Sock Only

Next Round: Knit.

Next Round: K-fb, knit to end of instep stitches; knit to last two heel stitches, k-fb, k1. Two stitches increased.

Repeat last two rounds an additional (D - E - 1) __7__ times. There are now (B x 2) __60__ stitches on the needles (if needed, insert any additional increases in the next round). Knit one round even.

Right Sock Only

Next Round: Knit.

Next Round: Knit to last two instep stitches, k-fb, k1; k1, k-fb, knit to end of heel stitches. Two stitches increased.

Repeat last two rounds an additional (D - E - 1) __7__ times. There are now (B x 2) __60__ stitches on the needles (if needed, insert any additional increases in the next round). Knit one round even.

———— ❖ ❖ ❖ ————

The Star Toe

If you're looking to add a little flair to your toe and don't demand a perfect fit, the star toe is a fun option. This toe is worked in a dome shape with increases spaced evenly around the circumference of the toe rather than lined up along the sides. This causes the increases to shoot out from the center point of the toe like the arms of a star.

The tip of this toe can be rounded a bit by increasing every round for the first $1/3$ of the increases. In general, this toe is best for the wearer who is willing to sacrifice fit for a little bit of style.

 *This toe is used in: **Sydney**, **Old-School Knee-Highs** and **Fjordland**.*

 ❖ ❖ ❖

Star Toe
Example Worksheet

Numbers Needed:

A **_60_** = number of stitches needed for foot

B **_44_** = number of stitches to increase, (A - 16)

C **_11_** = number of full increase rounds, (B ÷ 4), rounded down to the nearest whole number

D **_0_** = leftover increases, [B - (C x 4)]

To Work:

Cast on six stitches, three on each of two circulars or dpns, leaving a 16" tail. Knit each stitch with both the working yarn and the tail, ending with 12 loops on the needles. Each of these loops will be knitted as a separate stitch on the first round of the toe.

If working on dpns, divide these stitches evenly across four dpns with three stitches on each needle. If working on circulars, place a marker in the center of each needle, dividing the stitches into groups of three.

Round 1: Knit.

Round 2: *K-fb, k2; repeat from * to end of round. 16 stitches.

Round 3: Knit.

Round 4: *K-fb, knit to marker; repeat from * to end of round. Four stitches increased.

Repeat Rounds 3 - 4 an additional (C - 1) **_10_** times. There are now [(C x 4) + 16] **_60_** stitches on the needles. Knit one round even.

If D is not 0, work one more increase round, spacing the leftover increases as follows:

- *1 leftover increase:* Place increase after 2nd or 4th marker.
- *2 leftover increases:* Place increases after 1st and 3rd markers.
- *3 leftover increases:* Place increases after 1st, 2nd and 3rd markers or 1st, 3rd and 4th markers.

 ❖ ❖ ❖

The Short-Row Toe

The short-row toe forms a nicely rounded toe cup and is made by working a series of shorter and shorter rows, then reversing the process to make a gentle trapezoid.

It's worked almost exactly the same on both toe-up and top-down socks, the only difference being that the sock is started rather than ended with the toe. It can be worked in stockinette stitch, reverse stockinette or garter stitch (knit every row).

 *This toe is used in: **Diamond Lucy**, **Great Plains**, **Candelabra** and **Peace Lily**.*

Short-Row Toe Example Worksheet

Numbers Needed:

A _30_ = half the number of stitches needed for foot

B _10_ = A ÷ 3

C _10_ = wrapped side stitches, B if B is a whole number, or adjust up or down according to check #1 in "Check That" section

D _10_ = unwrapped center stitches, B if B is a whole number, or adjust up or down according to check #1 in "Check That" section

Check That:

1. Ensure that [(2 x C) + D] = A. Adjust C and D by a stitch in either direction to get the formula to work. Your goal is to get an equal number of wrapped stitches (C) on either side of the unwrapped center stitches (D), i.e. if A = 30, C and D both equal 10; if A = 32, C = 11 and D = 10.

2. If you have a narrow toe footprint, decrease D and increase C. If you have a wide toe footprint, increase D and decrease C, always making sure the formula above totals up.

To Work:

Cast on A _30_ stitches on each of two circulars or dpns or (A x 2) _60_ stitches total. The first (instep) needle holds the toe stitches, which are worked back and forth until the toe is complete. The stitches on the second (heel) needle are held until it is time to work the foot.

Shape Bottom of Toe

Row 1 (RS): Knit to last stitch on first needle, W&T (see glossary).

Row 2 (WS): Purl to last stitch on first needle, W&T.

Row 3: Knit to the stitch before the first wrapped stitch you come to, W&T.

Row 4: Purl to the stitch before the first wrapped stitch you come to, W&T.

Repeat the previous two rows until C _10_ stitches are wrapped on either side of D _10_ unwrapped center stitches.

Shape Top of Toe

Row 1 (RS): Knit to first wrapped stitch (do not knit across any wrapped stitches), lift wrap RS (see glossary), turn.

Row 2 (WS): Sl1, purl to first wrapped stitch (do not purl across any wrapped stitches), lift wrap WS, turn.

Row 3: Sl1, knit to next wrapped stitch (just past the stitch unwrapped on the previous RS row), lift wrap RS, turn.

Row 4: Sl1, purl to next wrapped stitch (just past the stitch unwrapped on the previous WS row), lift wrap WS, turn.

Repeat the previous two rows an additional (C - 3) _7_ times until a single wrapped stitch remains on either side.

Next Round: Sl1, knit to last wrapped stitch, lift wrap RS, but do not turn. If working on dpns, divide the stitches evenly across four dpns. Knit across the heel stitches to complete the round.

Next Round: Lift the final wrap (which is at the beginning of the instep needle) RS, then knit the rest of the round even.

These final two rounds help to eliminate those irritating gaps that can form at the corners of short-row toes and heels. By starting to work in the round before all the wraps have been lifted, these gaps seem to magically disappear.

A Word About Short Rows.
There are several different methods of wrapping and unwrapping short rows. The glossary demonstrates the method I've developed after much trial-and-error and piecing together of others' techniques. However, if you don't like the way these short rows look or you're having trouble making them look the same on both sides of your toe or heel, check the Bibliography for a list of great sock resource books. **Simple Socks Plain or Fancy** *by Priscilla Gibson-Roberts is an excellent choice, or Google "short-row heels" for dozens of other options.*

Chapter 4
Toe-Up Heels

Sock aficionados often remark that turning a heel is like magic. This is the point at which the sock really takes shape, and in a toe-up sock, once you're done with the heel, you're almost to the finish line.

Because the heel is such a crucial part of the sock, it is essential to a good fit. I encourage you to play around with these heels and seek out other toe-up heels to play with. Once you've found one (or several) that you like, use them in all your socks. Certain heels tend to fit certain feet better, and you are the best judge of what meets your needs.

Dummy Heels? *I teach a fit class where students use worsted-weight yarn and size 5 needles to make a series of "dummy heels" using each of the heel techniques in this chapter.*

Each student goes home with a sample heel that they can actually try on to determine how well it fits their foot. I encourage you to do the same using the worksheets in this book - it's a great way to see how each heel fits.

The Short-Row Heel

The short-row heel is a very common heel in toe-up sock patterns and it's especially good for people with low insteps.

Another benefit of the short-row heel is its ability to allow color patterns to flow uninterrupted from the foot to the leg. For this reason, I use it in many of my colorwork designs, both toe-up and top-down.

This heel is used in: Mix-and-Match Rib Sock Recipe, Sydney, Fjordland, Great Plains, Spring in Oregon and Peace Lily.

❖ ❖ ❖

Short-Row Heel Example Worksheet

Numbers Needed:

A __30__ = heel stitches, generally half of the total number of sock stitches

B __10__ = A ÷ 3

C __10__ = wrapped side stitches, B if B is a whole number, or adjust up or down according to check #1 in "Check That" section

D __10__ = unwrapped center stitches, B if B is a whole number, or adjust up or down according to check #1 in "Check That" section

E __2"__ = heel length in inches, (C x 2 ÷ rows per inch), rounded up to nearest $\frac{1}{4}$"

Check That:

1. Ensure that [(2 x C) + D = A]. Adjust C and D by a stitch in either direction to get the formula to work. Your goal is to get an equal number of wrapped stitches (C) on either side of the unwrapped center stitches (D), i.e. if A = 30, C and D both equal 10; if A = 32, C = 11 and D = 10.

2. If you have a narrow heel, decrease D and increase C. If you have a wide heel, increase D and decrease C, always making sure the formula in check #1 totals up.

To Work:

Start heel when foot measures E __2"__ less than desired finished length from tip of toe. Place A __30__ stitches on a single needle (the heel needle) and begin working back and forth across these stitches.

Shape Bottom of Heel

Row 1 (RS): Knit to last stitch on first needle, W&T (see glossary).

Row 2 (WS): Purl to last stitch on first needle, W&T.

Row 3: Knit to the stitch before the first wrapped stitch you come to, W&T.

Row 4: Purl to the stitch before the first wrapped stitch you come to, W&T.

Repeat the previous two rows until C __10__ stitches are wrapped on either side of D __10__ unwrapped center stitches.

Shape Top of Heel

Row 1 (RS): Knit to first wrapped stitch (do not knit across any wrapped stitches), lift wrap RS (see glossary), turn.

Row 2 (WS): Sl1, purl to first wrapped stitch (do not purl across any wrapped stitches), lift wrap WS, turn.

Row 3: Sl1, knit to next wrapped stitch (just past the stitch unwrapped on the previous RS row), lift wrap RS, turn.

Row 4: Sl1, purl to next wrapped stitch (just past the stitch unwrapped on the previous WS row), lift wrap WS, turn.

Repeat the previous two rows an additional (C - 3) __7__ times until a single wrapped stitch remains on either side.

Next Row: Sl1, knit to last wrapped stitch, lift wrap RS, but do not turn - you will be at the start of the instep stitches. If working on dpns, re-divide the heel stitches across two dpns.

Next Round: Work across the instep stitches in pattern; lift the final wrap (which is at the beginning of the heel needle) RS, then knit across the remaining heel stitches.

—————— ❖ ❖ ❖ ——————

The Hybrid Heel

This is a combination short-row heel and slip-stitch (aka heel stitch) heel flap with gusset to accommodate a higher instep.

You will need to start the gusset much sooner than the other heels, so be sure to adjust accordingly when using this heel.

 *This heel is used in: **Gull Wing**, **Diamond Lucy**, **Vortex**, **Sakura**, and **Candelabra**.*

—————— ❖ ❖ ❖ ——————
 ## Hybrid Heel Example Worksheet

Numbers Needed:

A _30_ = heel stitches, generally half of the total number of sock stitches

B _10_ = A ÷ 3

C _10_ = wrapped side stitches, B if B is a whole number, or adjust up or down according to check #1 in "Check That" section

D _10_ = unwrapped center stitches, B if B is a whole number, or adjust up or down according to check #1 in "Check That" section

E _15_ = gusset stitches, (A ÷ 2), rounded up if not a whole number

F _4 1/2"_ = heel length in inches, ([(E x 2) + (C x 2)] ÷ rows per inch), rounded up to nearest 1/4"

Check That:

1. Ensure that [(2 x C) + D] = A. Adjust C and D by a stitch in either direction to get the formula to work. Your goal is to get an equal number of wrapped stitches (C) on either side of the unwrapped center stitches (D), i.e. if A = 30, C and D both equal 10; if A = 32, C = 11 and D = 10.

2. If you have a narrow heel, decrease D and increase C. If you have a wide heel, increase D and decrease C, always making sure the formula in check #1 totals up.

3. If you have a high instep or you're having trouble fitting a sock over your heel, increase E by 1 to 4 stitches.

To Work:
Gusset

Start gusset when foot measures F _4 1/2"_ less than desired finished length from tip of toe.

Round 1: Work across instep stitches in pattern; k-fb, knit to last 2 heel stitches, k-fb, k1.

Round 2: Work across instep stitches in pattern; knit heel stitches.

Repeat Rounds 1-2 an additional (E - 2) *13* times, then work Round 1 once more. You will now have [(2 x E) + A] *60* heel stitches. Place a stitch marker on each side of the heel to separate the gusset stitches from the center heel stitches (the gusset markers will be E *15* stitches from either side of the heel).

Shape Bottom of Heel

Row 1 (RS): Knit to stitch before the 2nd gusset marker ([A + E - 1] *44* stitches), W&T.

Row 2 (WS): Purl to stitch before the 1st gusset marker ([A - 2] *28* stitches), W&T.

Row 3: Knit to the stitch before the first wrapped stitch you come to, W&T.

Row 4: Purl to the stitch before the first wrapped stitch you come to, W&T.

Repeat the previous two rows until C *10* stitches are wrapped on either side of D *10* unwrapped center stitches.

Next Round: With RS facing, knit to end of heel stitches, lifting wraps RS as you encounter them, then work across instep stitches in pattern to bring you back to the start of the heel.

Work Heel Flap

Row 1 (RS): Knit E *15* stitches, then knit (A - 1) *29* lifting remaining wraps RS as you encounter them. You should now be one stitch before the second gusset marker. Remove marker and SSK the stitches that were on either side of the marker, turn.

Row 2 (WS): [Sl1, p1] to stitch before marker (if A is an even number then end with sl1, otherwise end with p1). You should now be one stitch before the first gusset marker. Remove marker and p2tog the stitches that were on either side of the marker, turn.

Row 3: Sl1, knit (A - 2) *28* , SSK, turn.

Row 4: [Sl1, p1] to stitch before gap formed by previous WS row's turn (if A is an even number then end with sl1, otherwise end with p1), p2tog, turn.

Repeat the previous two rows an additional (E - 3) *12* times, then work Row 3 once more, but do not turn - you will be slowly working up the edge of the gusset and forming the heel flap as you go.

Next Round: Work across instep stitches in pattern; k2tog, knit to end of heel.

As with the short-row toe and heel, eliminating the last gusset stitch on the first round of the leg will help prevent holes at the join between the heel and the leg.

Afterthought Heel

This heel is worked after the main body of the sock is done. If you tend to wear through your sock heels quickly, you'll love this method because you can easily rip out an afterthought heel and replace it as needed.

It also shares the short-row heel's benefit of allowing uninterrupted color patterns to flow from the foot to the leg.

You'll need some waste yarn for this technique and a fondness for Kitchener stitch. (You can work this heel exactly the same way in a top-down sock.)

This heel is used in: **Snuggalicious Slipper Socks**, **Syncopated Rib Boot Socks**, **Old-School Knee-Highs** and **The Dude Abides**.

❖ ❖ ❖

 ## Afterthought Heel Example Worksheet

Numbers Needed:

A <u>30</u> = number of heel stitches; generally half of the total number of sock stitches

B <u>62</u> = total stitches after waste yarn is removed, [(A + 1) x 2]

C <u>15</u> = A ÷ 2

D <u>2$^1/_4$"</u> = heel length in inches, ([(B ÷ 2) - (C ÷ 2)] ÷ rows per inch), rounded up to nearest $^1/_4$"

To Work:

When foot measures approximately D <u>2$^1/_4$"</u> less than desired finished length from tip of toe, pick up a piece of scrap/waste yarn and use it to knit across the heel stitches. Then, drop the waste yarn, go back to the start of the heel, pick up the working yarn and knit across the waste yarn stitches.

Continue knitting the leg of your sock with the working yarn - the waste yarn holds the stitches where the heel will eventually go.

When it's time to make your heel, go back and carefully pick up the stitches held by the waste yarn across the top and bottom of the heel. There will be an extra stitch on the top needle.

Pick up one more stitch in a corner of the heel with the bottom needle so that there is an equal number of stitches on both needles or B <u>62</u> total.

Place a marker at each side of the heel to indicate where the heel cup decreases will go (‖ indicates the location of the marker in the following instructions). Remove waste yarn.

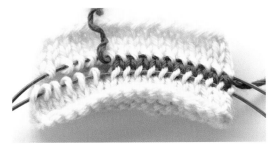

Join yarn to be used for heel in either corner.

Round 1: Knit.

Round 2: K1, SSK, knit to 3 stitches before first side marker, k2tog, k1 || k1, SSK, knit to 3 stitches before second side marker, k2tog, k1 ||.

Repeat these two rounds until there are C _15_ or fewer stitches left or until the heel is about D _2¼"_ deep.

You may not be able to get exactly to C, but close is good enough. In this case, when C = 15 and B = 62, you'll end up with 14 stitches left after doing your last decrease round.

 Pointy Heel? If you find that the heel as calculated is too pointy, eliminate the plain knit round (Round 1) between the last two or three decrease rounds. Putting the decreases on every round instead of every other will help to round out the back of the heel cup.

Place the stitches between each marker on a single needle (i.e. top-of-heel stitches on one needle, bottom-of-heel stitches on another) and graft the heel cup closed using Kitchener Stitch (see glossary).

❖ ❖ ❖

Star Heel Variation of Afterthought Heel

To give your afterthought heel a little more pizazz, you can work it in a star decrease pattern.

B must be divisible by 4 for this heel. If needed, pick up extra stitches in the corners where the heel meets the instep (in our example, we'd increase so that B = 64), and then place markers every (B ÷ 4) _16_ stitches.

Join yarn to be used for heel.

Round 1: Knit.

Round 2: *Knit to 2 stitches before marker, k2tog; repeat from * an additional 3 times.

Work as for a regular afterthought heel, substituting these rounds for Rounds 1 and 2 of afterthought heel instructions.

Chapter 5
Finishing

After you've knit your sock leg, all you need to do is bind off the stitches and weave in the ends. Easy, right? Well...toe-up bind-offs can be a challenge. A regular bind-off is just not flexible enough to accommodate the amount of stretch to which a sock cuff is subjected.

The three bind-offs included in this chapter are the best I've found so far. I've listed my favorite first, and use it nearly all of the time. As always, I encourage you to explore and see which bind-offs work best for you.

Yarn Over Bind-Off

I love this bind-off, which I learned from Eunny Jang, *Interweave Knits* editor and all-around knitting guru.

It creates a lovely, stretchy edge that has a decorative crocheted quality. This is the most flexible bind-off I've encountered and I wouldn't make knee-highs with any other finish. It's also great for lace shawls, kids' sweater neckbands and any other edge that needs a greater-than-usual amount of stretch.

Here's How:

At the start of your bind-off round, knit a stitch, YO, then knit another stitch.

You'll have three loops on the right-hand needle.

*Insert the tip of the left needle under both the YO and the right-most stitch and lift them over the left-hand stitch and off the needle. YO and knit another stitch. Repeat from * until all stitches are bound off.

If you find that you're having trouble getting the stitches to cooperate, grab a small crochet hook and use it instead. The movement is slightly different in that you're pulling the left-hand loop through rather than lifting the other loops over, but the hook makes all the difference in getting those stitches to behave themselves.

After you fasten off, you can smooth out the bound-off edge by making a "false chain" that connects the last bind-off stitch to the first as follows:

First, find the first stitch of your bind-off and locate the "chain" at the top of that stitch. Thread the tip of the yarn needle under both legs of that chain starting on the right side.

Pull the yarn tail through, and then go back to the last chain of the bind-off round. Thread the tip of the needle back down through the center of that chain (the same spot where the tail comes up).

Pull the yarn through, matching the tension of the rest of the bind-off round. Weave the tail in securely on the wrong side of the work to finish.

Fasten Off! *When you're done knitting, do you cut your working yarn and then simply pull on the loop until the tail pops through the last bound-off stitch? Or do you thread the tail through that last loop and pull it tight? If you're using option #2, you're putting a needless knot at the end of your bind-off. Next time, pull out that last stitch so that it forms a nice big loop, cut the yarn so that you'll have about a 6" tail, and pull on the loop instead*

of the cut end of the yarn until your tail pops through. It won't unravel, I promise, and you've just eliminated a knot from your knitting - always a good thing in my book!

Sewn Bind-Off

This is a well-known bind-off for toe-up socks, generally credited to knitting trailblazer Elizabeth Zimmermann. I find that it looks particularly nice when used to finish off a k1, p1 rib.

Here's How:

When you're ready to bind off, cut the yarn, leaving a tail that's about three times the circumference of your sock.

Thread this tail onto a yarn needle and proceed as follows, pulling the yarn tail taut but not tight at the end of each step:

Step 1: Thread the yarn tail through the first two stitches on the left needle as if to purl, leaving both stitches on the needle.

Step 2: Thread the yarn tail through the right-most stitch on the left needle as if to knit. Slip it onto the back needle so that it's now at the end of the round.

Step 3: Repeat Step 1.

Step 4: Thread the yarn tail through the right-most stitch on the left needle as if to knit, slipping it off the needle in the process.

Repeat Steps 3 and 4 until one stitch remains (this is the stitch that was moved to the right needle in Step 2). Slip this stitch off the needle and fasten off.

P2tog Bind-Off

Although not as flexible as the yarn over or sewn bind-offs, this method still produces a nice stretchy edge and is great for situations where not as much stretch is required, such as on an ankle-length sock or ruffled edge.

Here's How:

At the start of your bind-off round, p2tog. *Slip stitch from right needle back to left needle and purl it together with the next stitch. Repeat from * to the end of the round and fasten off.

Weaving In Ends

The final step in finishing the sock, after all stitches are bound off, is to weave in your ends. If they're not already on the wrong side of your knitting, use a yarn needle to thread them through. Turn your sock inside out and weave these ends securely for a couple of inches.

It's important to attempt to match the stretch of the fabric when you're weaving in ends, particularly on the cuff. If you weave the end too tightly, it will create a tight spot in your sock where the stitches don't stretch.

When weaving ends at the toe or heel, thread the yarn through the fronts of the stitches (as viewed from the wrong side) following a snake-like path.

When weaving in the end at the cuff, my go-to method is to find a column of ribbing and weave the tail back and forth through the vertical knit stitches.

Make sure you weave a long enough length of yarn that it won't pull out after significant wear.

Caring For Your Socks

After putting all that hard work into making your socks, you want them to last. Sock care is pretty easy once you get a routine down, although if your house is like mine, you will need to keep your socks out of the regular laundry basket in case your husband decides to throw everything into the washer and dryer without separating your precious knitting out first.

Most socks can go into the washing machine's cold cycle, but when in doubt, hand wash them. You don't want to put anything but the most heavy-duty (i.e. acrylic) socks in the dryer, so set up a little air-drying area in your laundry room or bathroom.

To easily hand-wash socks, get a bottle of specially-formulated wool wash (such as Soak or Eucalan) that doesn't require rinsing. Fill a basin or large bowl with cool water and a squirt of the wool wash, swish the socks around until they're saturated, and let them soak for 10-20 minutes.

Then, throw them in your empty washing machine on the spin cycle or roll them in a towel to squeeze out most of the water. (Amy, my technical editor, uses her salad spinner.) Shake out, and hang or lay flat on a towel to dry.

If you're giving a pair of socks as a gift or will be showing them off without a foot in them, you may want to block them on a pair of sock blockers.

These are flat, sock-shaped forms with cut-outs to allow air circulation. Fiber Trends sells a blue plastic version that I've used for years with great success.

There are also a number of small artisans who hand-carve wooden sock blockers, often with fun cut-out designs. If you're budget-minded, you can make your own using wire coat hangers - simply bend the hanger so that it approximates a nice sock shape, stretch your damp socks over it and hang it by the hook to dry.

Blocking is not necessary for socks, since they're immediately stretched out of shape by your feet, but it's a nice way to present them if you're giving them as a gift (or photographing them for your blog).

Chapter 6
Advanced Techniques

Once you've got the basics down, there are a few things you can learn that will help take your sock knitting to the next level. We'll explore four areas of advanced sock technique in this chapter (the first two of which can be applied to all areas of your knitting).

Reading Charts

In my many encounters with knitters, it seems that there are those who love charts and those who refuse to use them. Often it boils down to individual learning style as well as knitting expertise, so it's not always the beginning knitters who don't like charts.

Even if you prefer the written word, there is value in learning the basics of chart reading. What charts offer that line-by-line written instructions don't is a graphic representation of the stitch pattern that spans both horizontal and vertical space.

Unless there's something really funky going on with increases and decreases (such as you'd find in a complex lace pattern), you can tell how your knitting is supposed to look by examining a chart. You can easily see how the stitches line up on top of each other, in addition to knowing what's next to what on a horizontal row.

In this book, I've included charts for all but the most basic of stitch patterns.

If you want to practice your chart reading, I recommend reading across a row of written instructions and then comparing it to what's on the chart. In this way, you'll start to see how the written-out stitches and the charted stitches go together. It's also a great way to double-check if you find yourself having trouble with a stitch instruction. Go to the other representation of the instructions, and compare the two.

All of my charts are written to represent the right side of the work, so on a piece that's worked flat, the same symbol is used to represent both the knit stitch when working a right side row and the purl stitch when working a wrong side row. This allows easy comparison between chart and knitted fabric, but can be a little confusing when working flat. Fortunately, socks are mainly worked in the round, so what you see on the chart is what you get when you're knitting. The few exceptions in this book are the cuff on the *Spring in Oregon* sock, and the patterned heel flaps on *Spring in Oregon* and *Sakura*, which are knitted flat.

Charts are read from bottom to top, starting on the right edge for right side rows and the left edge for wrong side rows. The row number is generally found on the edge where you are to begin knitting, so right side row numbers are found on the right edge and wrong side row numbers on the left edge.

When knitting top-down socks, the stitch pattern will be upside-down compared to how it is represented on the chart. With toe-up knitting, however, the way it's charted is the way it will turn out.

Take a look at the charts in this book and, even if you don't knit from them, compare your finished sock to the chart. Can you see how the stitch pattern is represented by the chart symbols? If you do, you've just taken your first step toward being a chart-reader.

Cable Techniques

You may be adept with a cable needle, but what do you do if you don't have one? Or if you're getting annoyed at the little two-stitch twists that I like to put in my designs? Is there an easier way than dealing with all of your sock needles, plus a cable needle? I'm happy to say that there is.

Cabling Without A Cable Needle

This technique comes in handy both when you find yourself without a cable needle (such as when you're knitting on a long car trip and your cable needle disappears into the depths of the no-man's land between the passenger seat and the center console) or when you're knitting lots of small cables worked over two to four stitches.

For these little cables, it's often more of a hassle to slide the stitches onto the cable needle and then knit them off again, than it is to just fly without a needle. If you can't bring yourself to go totally needle-free, check out the next section for another little trick I've learned.

To cable without a needle, you need to take a little leap of faith and actually drop live stitches off of your needles. It's not as scary as it sounds, really!

Here are the steps for a C4F, which normally would involve slipping two stitches to a cable needle, holding them in front, knitting two stitches from the left needle, then knitting the two stitches from the cable needle to get a 2 over 2 twist.

Step 1: Slip the tip of the right needle into the backs of the 3rd and 4th stitches on the left needle.

Step 2: Pinch the base of the four stitches involved in the cable tightly with your left thumb and index finger. Slip the first two stitches off of the left needle and let them "pop" to the front.

Step 3: Disturbing the off-needle stitches as little as possible, slide the 3rd and 4th stitches that are currently on both needles onto the right needle and off the left. Slip the tip of the left needle into the two loose stitches.

To do a C4B (crossing in the opposite direction), slip the tip of the right needle into the fronts of the 3rd and 4th stitches and let the loose stitches pop to the back instead of the front.

Step 4: Slide the first two stitches on the right needle back to the left needle, to the right of the recaptured stitches. You will see that you now have your cable twist in place right beneath the left needle.

Step 5: Knit these four stitches and voila! Cable!

You can translate these directions to pretty much any cable crossing you can come up with, apart from extremely complex cables that involve two cable needles (such as a Gordian Knot). It's also not the best choice for extremely wide cables, such as an eight-stitch cross, unless you're really confident in your loose stitch-grabbing abilities.

Cabling With a Locking Stitch Marker

If dropping stitches and picking them back up makes you quiver in your boots, I've got another method for small cables (two to four stitches) that can eliminate the hassle of a full-size cable needle.

Pick up a locking stitch marker. Instead of placing the stitch(es) on a cable needle, slip them onto the open marker.

Work the required stitch(es) from the left needle.

Slip the stitch(es) from the open stitch marker back to the left needle.

Work the stitch(es) from the left needle instead of from a cable needle.

This method involves only one extra move (slipping the stitch(es) back to the left needle) and avoids the potential tangles that a full-sized cable needle can cause. I use this constantly with my traveling stitch designs.

Converting from Top-Down to Toe-Up

Once you've fallen in love with knitting toe-up socks, how do you convert traditional top-down patterns to start at the toe? It's not always as easy as it might sound, but since you were smart enough to buy this book, you'll have a head start!

When knitting a sock starting at the opposite end, you will need to reverse the construction of the toe, heel and any stitch patterns.

If you're converting a relatively basic sock, you should easily be able to determine how many stitches are in the foot and/or leg. Use these numbers to calculate your favorite toe and heel, using the worksheets in Chapter 8.

For a more complicated sock, you'll need to determine if the stitch pattern looks the same when knit from the opposite direction. To do this, turn a picture of the sock you're planning to knit upside-down. Does it look the same? If so, you can knit from the stitch pattern directions as written in the pattern. If not, you'll need to decide if you can live with how the pattern looks upside-down.

Often a stitch pattern will look different (but delightful) when it's turned on its head and, if it's acceptable in its new orientation, you can knit directly from the pattern directions in this case as well.

What do you do if you REALLY want the pattern to look the same as in the top-down pattern? My first answer would be that you should just give in and knit this sock from the top down. Really, it's okay!

If you're absolutely insistent that you need to knit this sock toe-up, you can attempt to chart the pattern in reverse. If the stitch pattern is not already charted, chart it out as written in the original sock design. Turn the chart upside-down, and re-chart it in reverse, swapping increases for decreases and vice-versa.

Cables are relatively easy to turn over. Lace patterns may or may not work, since increases and decreases don't look exactly alike.

Knitting Two Socks At Once

Do you suffer from Single Sock Syndrome? This dreaded malady strikes when the first sock comes off the needles and the knitter realizes there is an entire second sock to knit, exactly like the one they just finished, to complete the pair.

If you're one of those folks with a knitting basket full of single socks, you need to learn this technique. There are several advantages to this method, the main one being that when you bind off, you'll have a completed pair of socks instead of just one.

The methods here are described for circular needles. You can't really knit two socks on the same set of needles when using dpns, so to you dpn fanatics, I will gently explain that if you'd like to knit two socks at once, you'll need to get a second set of needles. Knit a round or two on the first sock, then set it aside and knit those same rounds on the second.

To knit two socks on two circulars, cast on your toe stitches for each sock using two different balls of yarn, one for each sock.

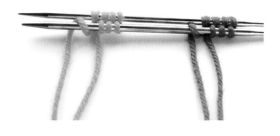

Start knitting around the socks in the following sequence, making sure to knit each sock with its own yarn - sock 1 instep, sock 2 instep, sock 2 heel, sock 1 heel (or, if the heel stitches come first in the sock pattern's sequence, work them as sock 1 heel, sock 2 heel, sock 2 instep, sock 1 instep). This completes one round.

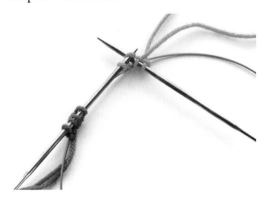

Everything that is done on one sock is also done on the other. When you reach the heel turn (the part that is worked back and forth), work the entire heel on the first sock before moving on to the second.

While you are working on one sock, the other rests to the side, out of the way (relatively speaking).

The main difficulty my students and I have with this method is keeping the two balls of yarn from getting horribly tangled up with the needles and each other. You need to spend some time figuring out the rhythm of untangling everything before each and every sock section so that you don't get completely tied up in knots.

My new favorite method for working two socks at once is on one long circular. I resisted learning to do this for a long time, since I don't generally enjoy knitting a single sock Magic Loop-style as much as on two circulars. I recently gave it a try, however, and found that I was much less apt to get myself tangled up when using a single circular because there weren't extra needle tips dangling in the way.

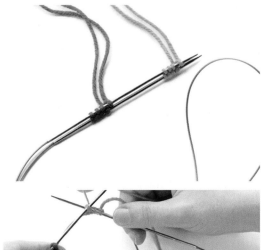

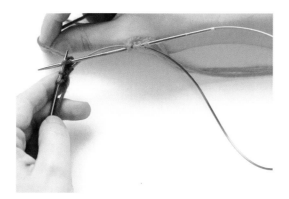

The sock sections are knit in the same sequence as on two circulars, but instead of letting one sock hang down while the other is being worked, both socks remain on the needle tips.

The biggest potential mishap with this method is knitting across both socks with the same ball of yarn, resulting in conjoined twins.

There are two recent books that discuss these methods in detail. They are great resources if you'd like to learn more about one of these methods and find patterns written specifically for knitting two socks at once. The first, *Knitting Circles Around Socks* by Antje Gillingham, addresses knitting on two circulars. The second, *2-at-a-Time Socks* by Melissa Morgan-Oakes, focuses on using a single long circular (the Magic Loop method).

Chapter 7
The Patterns

Now that we've gotten all that learning out of the way, it's time to have some fun knitting socks! This chapter is divided into two parts, each with different types of socks. The first section, *Family Socks*, includes patterns designed for a wide range of knitting abilities and foot sizes. With the patterns in the second section, *Fancy Socks*, you can show off your knitting prowess with a selection of patterns utilizing cables, texture, traveling stitches and lace. Due to the complexity of the stitch patterns, the designs in the *Fancy Socks* section are sized to fit a Women's M foot ($7^1/_2$" to $8^1/_2$" in circumference). If you need help resizing, please see Chapter 1.

Family Socks

Fancy Socks

	Non-Shaped Round Toe	Shaped Round Toe	Anatomical Toe	Star Toe	Short-Row Toe	Short-Row Heel	Hybrid Heel	Afterthought Heel
Snuggalicious Slipper Socks		x						x
Mix-and-Match Sock Recipe	x					x		
Syncopated Rib Boot Socks			x					x
Old-School Knee-Highs				x				x*
Gull Wing	x						x	
Sydney				x		x		
Fjordland				x		x		
Diamond Lucy					x		x	
The Dude Abides			x					x
Candelabra					x		x	
Vortex		x					x	
Great Plains					x	x		
Spring in Oregon	x					x		
Peace Lily					x	x		
Sakura	x						x	

This grid indicates which patterns use the toes and heels described in Chapters 3 and 4 of this book so that you can easily find the ones that use your favorites. Of course, you are encouraged to use the worksheets in Chapter 8 to mix-and-match!

x* indicates that this pattern uses the star variation of the afterthought heel

Family Socks

Snuggalicious Slipper Socks

If you need a quick gift for someone, these chunky-weight slipper socks knit up lightning fast and come in seven sizes. Optional contrasting toes, heels and cuffs add some fun to a very simple pattern.

Materials:

Approximately 50 (75, 75, 100, 100, 150, 200) yards chunky-weight yarn in MC and 35 (50, 50, 75, 75, 100, 100) yards in CC for 2-color socks or 85 (125, 125, 175, 175, 250, 300) yards chunky-weight yarn for solid-color socks

Samples use Lorna's Laces Shepherd Bulky (100% superwash wool) in Edgewater for solid-color child's socks and Brown Sheep Lamb's Pride Bulky (85% wool, 15% mohair) in RPM Pink (MC) and Kiwi (CC) for 2-color women's socks.

US5 (3.75mm) needles or size needed to obtain gauge

Gauge:

5 stitches/7 rounds per inch in stockinette stitch

Sizes:

Foot circumference = approximately 5 (6, 7, 8, 9, 10, 11)"

Toe

Using your favorite toe-up method, cast on 2 (3, 3, 4, 4, 5, 5) instep stitches and 2 (3, 3, 4, 4, 5, 5) heel stitches with CC, dividing them across your selected needles.

Note: If using a single color of yarn, use in place of both MC and CC throughout without breaking.

Place a marker at the start of the instep stitches to indicate the beginning of the round.

Round 1: K-fb, knit to last two instep stitches, k-fb, k1; repeat across heel stitches. 8 (10, 10, 12, 12, 14, 14) stitches.

Repeat Round 1 an additional 1 (1, 2, 2, 2, 3, 3) times. 12 (14, 18, 20, 20, 26, 26) stitches.

Next Round: K-fb, knit to last two instep stitches, k-fb, k1; repeat across heel stitches. 16 (18, 22, 24, 24, 30, 30) stitches.

Next Round: Knit.

Repeat last two rounds an additional 2 (3, 3, 4, 5, 5, 6) times. 24 (30, 34, 40, 44, 50, 54) stitches. Break CC.

Foot

With MC, work until the foot from the tip of the toe to the needles measures approximately 1 1/2 (1 3/4, 2, 2 1/4, 2 1/2, 2 3/4, 3)" less than the desired total length.

Heel

Hold Stitches for Heel

Knit across instep stitches. With waste yarn, knit across heel stitches. Drop waste yarn and go back to start of heel. Knit across heel stitches with working yarn.

Leg

Continuing in the round, work four rounds even with MC. Break MC and join CC. Work in k1, p1 rib for four rounds. Bind off all stitches using your favorite toe-up method. (I used the p2tog bind-off.)

Insert Afterthought Heel

Carefully pick up the stitches held by the waste yarn, placing the back-of-leg stitches on one needle and the bottom-of-foot stitches on another. There will be an extra stitch on the top (back-of-leg) needle, so pick up a stitch in the corner of the heel with the other needle so that there are 13 (16, 18, 21, 23, 26, 28) stitches on each needle. If working on dpns, divide each set of stitches over two dpns.

Join CC at corner of heel at the point where the bottom-of-foot stitches and the back-of-leg stitches meet and begin working in the round on these 26 (32, 36, 42, 46, 52, 56) stitches.

Round 1: Knit.

Round 2: *K1, SSK, knit to three stitches before corner of heel, k2tog, k1; repeat from *.

Repeat Rounds 1 & 2 until 6 (8, 8, 10, 10, 12, 12) stitches remain. Graft the heel closed from corner to corner using Kitchener stitch.

Mix-and-Match Rib Sock Recipe

This sock recipe is great for mastering the basics of toe-up socks and can be used as a starting point for practicing the toe and heel worksheets in the back of this book. It's also sized to fit just about anyone. Don't be afraid to play around with it!

Materials:

Approximately 80 (125, 150, 250, 325, 400, 450, 475) yards sport-weight yarn

Samples use Dale of Norway Baby Ull (100% merino wool) in 5303 for baby socks, Louet Gems Sport (100% merino wool) in Mourning Dove for toddler socks, Debbie Bliss Baby Cashmerino (55% merino wool, 33% microfiber, 12% cashmere) in Dusty Lavender for child's socks, Fleece Artist Casbah (80% merino wool, 10% cashmere, 10% nylon) in Vintage for women's socks and Dream in Color Smooshy (100% merino wool) in Good Luck Jade for men's socks.

US2 (2.75mm) needles or size needed to obtain gauge

Gauge:

8 stitches/11 rounds per inch in stockinette stitch

Sizes:

Foot circumference = approximately 4 (5, 6, 7, 8, 9, 10, 11)"

Toe

Using your favorite toe-up method, cast on 4 (6, 6, 8, 8, 10, 10, 12) instep stitches and 4 (6, 6, 8, 8, 10, 10, 12) heel stitches, dividing them across your selected needles. Place a marker at the start of the instep stitches to indicate the beginning of the round.

Round 1: K-fb, knit to last two instep stitches, k-fb, k1; repeat across heel stitches. 12 (16, 16, 20, 20, 24, 24, 28) stitches.

Round 2: Knit.

Repeat Rounds 1 & 2 an additional 4 (5, 7, 8, 10, 11, 13, 14) times. 28 (36, 44, 52, 60, 68, 76, 84) stitches. 14 (18, 22, 26, 30, 34, 38, 42) on each needle.

Foot

Begin working the instep stitches in your chosen rib pattern from written instructions below while continuing to work the heel stitches in stockinette stitch. Work until the foot from the tip of the toe to the needles measures approximately 1 (1, 1¹⁄₂, 1¹⁄₂, 1³⁄₄, 2, 2¹⁄₄, 2¹⁄₂)" less than the desired total length.

Basic K2, P2 Rib Pattern for Instep:
(over multiple of 4 stitches + 2 and 1 round)
Round 1: *P2, k2; repeat from * to last two instep stitches, p2.

Bamboo Rib Pattern for Instep:
(over multiple of 4 stitches + 2 and 4 rounds)
Rounds 1 & 2: *P2, k2; repeat from * to last two instep stitches, p2.
Round 3: Purl all stitches.
Round 4: Repeat Round 1.

Garter Rib Pattern for Instep:
(over multiple of 4 stitches + 2 and 2 rounds)
Round 1: *P2, k2; repeat from * to last two instep stitches, p2.
Round 2: Knit all stitches.

Eyelet Rib Pattern for Instep:

(over multiple of 4 stitches + 2 and 4 rounds)

Round 1: *P2, k2; repeat from * to last two instep stitches, p2.

Round 2: *P2, k2tog, YO; repeat from * to last two instep stitches, p2.

Round 3: Repeat Round 1.

Round 4: *P2, YO, SSK; repeat from * to last two instep stitches, p2.

Cable Rib Pattern for Instep

(over multiple of 4 stitches + 2 and 4 rounds)

Rounds 1 & 2: *P2, k2; repeat from * to last two instep stitches, p2.

Round 3: *P2, C2B; repeat from * to last two instep stitches, p2.

Round 4: Repeat Round 1.

Hourglass Rib Pattern for Instep:

(over multiple of 4 stitches + 2 and 4 rounds)

Round 1: *P2, k2; repeat from * to last two instep stitches, p2.

Round 2: *P2, k2tog-tbl leaving stitches on left needle, then knit the same two stitches together through front loops and slip them off the needle; repeat from * to last two instep stitches, p2.

Round 3: *P2, k1, YO, k1; repeat from * to last two instep stitches, p2.

Round 4: *P2, SSK, k1; repeat from * to last two instep stitches, p2.

Heel

Work across instep stitches in pattern. The heel will be worked back and forth on the 14 (18, 22, 26, 30, 34, 38, 42) heel stitches.

Shape Bottom of Heel

Row 1 (RS): Knit to last stitch on needle, W&T.

Row 2: Purl to last stitch on needle, W&T.

Row 3: Knit to stitch before wrapped stitch (do not knit across any wrapped stitches), W&T.

Row 4: Purl to stitch before wrapped stitch (do not purl across any wrapped stitches), W&T.

Repeat Rows 3 & 4 an additional 3 (4, 6, 7, 8, 10, 11, 12) times - there are now 5 (6, 8, 9, 10, 12, 13, 14) wrapped stitches on either side of 4 (6, 6, 8, 10, 10, 12, 14) unwrapped center stitches.

Shape Top of Heel

Row 1 *(RS):* Knit to first wrapped stitch (do not knit across any wrapped stitches), lift wrap RS, turn.

Row 2 *(WS):* Sl1, purl to first wrapped stitch (do not purl across any wrapped stitches), lift wrap WS, turn.

Row 3: Sl1, knit to next wrapped stitch (just past the stitch unwrapped on the previous RS row), lift wrap RS, turn.

Row 4: Sl1, purl to next wrapped stitch (just past the stitch unwrapped on the previous WS row), lift wrap WS, turn.

Repeat Rows 3 & 4 an additional 2 (3, 5, 6, 7, 9, 10, 11) times - a single wrapped stitch remains on either side of heel.

Next Row: Sl1, knit to last wrapped stitch, lift wrap RS, but do not turn. You should be at the beginning of the instep stitches.

Next Round: Work instep stitches in pattern as established; lift wrap RS, knit to end of heel stitches.

Leg

Continuing in the round, work the instep stitches in pattern as established and the heel/back-of-leg stitches as follows below. Be sure to work the same round across the back of the leg as you just worked across the instep. If you're feeling adventurous, be creative and put a different rib up the back of the leg than is on the front!

End when ribbed portion of leg measures approximately 2 (3, 4, 5, 6, 7, 8, 8)" from top of heel or desired finished length. Bind off all stitches using your favorite toe-up method. (I used the yarn over bind-off.)

Basic K2, P2 Rib Pattern for Back of Leg:
(over multiple of 4 stitches + 2 and 1 round)
Round 1: *K2, p2; repeat from * to last two heel stitches, k2.

Bamboo Rib Pattern for Back of Leg:
(over multiple of 4 stitches + 2 and 4 rounds)
Rounds 1 & 2: *K2, p2; repeat from * to last two heel stitches, k2.
Round 3: Purl all stitches.
Round 4: Repeat Round 1.

Garter Rib Pattern for Back of Leg:
(over multiple of 4 stitches + 2 and 2 rounds)
Round 1: *K2, p2; repeat from * to last two heel stitches, k2.
Round 2: Knit all stitches.

Eyelet Rib Pattern for Back of Leg:
(over multiple of 4 stitches + 2 and 4 rounds)
Round 1: *K2, p2; repeat from * to last two heel stitches, k2.
Round 2: *K2tog, YO, p2; repeat from * to last two heel stitches, k2tog, YO.
Round 3: Repeat Round 1.
Round 4: *YO, SSK, p2; repeat from * to last two heel stitches, YO, SSK.

Cable Rib Pattern for Back of Leg:
(over multiple of 4 stitches + 2 and 4 rounds)
Rounds 1 & 2: *K2, p2; repeat from * to last two heel stitches, k2.
Round 3: *C2B, p2; repeat from * to last two heel stitches, k2.
Round 4: Repeat Round 1.

Hourglass Rib Pattern for Back of Leg:
(over multiple of 4 stitches + 2 and 4 rounds)
Round 1: *K2, p2; repeat from * to last two heel stitches, k2.

Round 2: *K2tog-tbl leaving stitches on left needle, then knit the same two stitches together through front loops and slip them off the needle, p2; repeat from * to last two heel stitches, k2tog-tbl leaving stitches on left needle, then knit the same two stitches together through front loops and slip them off the needle.
Round 3: *K1, YO, k1, p2; repeat from * to last two heel stitches, k1, YO, k1.
Round 4: *SSK, k1, p2; repeat from * to last two heel stitches, SSK, k1.

Toe-Up!

Syncopated Rib Boot Socks

This is a simple worsted-weight ribbed sock with a slight twist on the ribbing pattern - instead of repeating a small sequence over and over (such as k1, p1 or k2, p2), this rib mimics the syncopated jazz beat of short-long-short. These are my husband's new favorite socks!

Materials:

Approximately 150 (200, 250, 275, 300, 350) yards worsted-weight yarn

Samples use Dream In Color Classy (100% merino wool) in Cool Fire for child's socks shown on p. 59 and Louet Gems Worsted (100% merino wool) in Navy for men's socks.

US3 (3.25mm) needles or size needed to obtain gauge

Gauge:

6 stitches/8 rounds per inch in stockinette stitch

Sizes:

Foot circumference = approximately 5 (6, 7, 8, 9, 10)"

Toe

Using your favorite toe-up method, cast on 4 (4, 6, 6, 7, 8) instep stitches and 4 (3, 6, 5, 7, 7) heel stitches, dividing them across your selected needles. Place a marker at the start of the instep stitches to indicate the beginning of the round.

Shape Inner Edge of Toe (both socks)
Round 1: K-fb, knit to last two instep stitches, k-fb, k1; repeat across heel stitches. 12 (11, 16, 15, 18, 19) stitches, 6 (6, 8, 8, 9, 10) instep and 6 (5, 8, 7, 9, 9) heel.

Repeat Round 1 an additional 2 (3, 4, 5, 6, 7) times. 20 (23, 32, 35, 42, 47) stitches, 10 (12, 16, 18, 21, 24) instep and 10 (11, 16, 17, 21, 23) heel.

Shape Outer Edge of Right Sock Toe
Round 1: Knit.
Round 2: Knit to last two instep stitches, k-fb, k1; k-fb, knit across remaining heel stitches. 22 (25, 34, 37, 44, 49) stitches, 11 (13, 17, 19, 22, 25) instep and 11 (12, 17, 18, 22, 24) heel.

Repeat Rounds 1 & 2 an additional 2 (4, 3, 5, 5, 6) times. 26 (33, 40, 47, 54, 61) stitches, 13 (17, 20, 24, 27, 31) instep and 13 (16, 20, 23, 27, 30) heel.

Next Round: Knit.
Next Round: Knit to last two instep stitches, k-fb, k1; knit across heel stitches. 27 (34, 41, 48, 55, 62) stitches, 14 (18, 21, 25, 28, 32) instep and 13 (16, 20, 23, 27, 30) heel.

Repeat the last two rounds once more. 28 (35, 42, 49, 56, 63) stitches, 15 (19, 22, 26, 29, 33) instep and 13 (16, 20, 23, 27, 30) heel. Knit one round even.

Shape Outer Edge of Left Sock Toe
Round 1: Knit.
Round 2: K-fb, knit across remaining instep stitches; knit to last two heel stitches, k-fb, k1. 22 (25, 34, 37, 44, 49) stitches, 11 (13, 17, 19, 22, 25) instep and 11 (12, 17, 18, 22, 24) heel.

Repeat Rounds 1 & 2 an additional 2 (4, 3, 5, 5, 6) times. 26 (33, 40, 47, 54, 61) stitches, 13 (17, 20, 24, 27, 31) instep and 13 (16, 20, 23, 27, 30) heel.

Next Round: Knit.
Next Round: K-fb, knit across remaining instep stitches; knit across heel stitches. 27 (34, 41, 48, 55, 62) stitches, 14 (18, 21, 25, 28, 32) instep and 13 (16, 20, 23, 27, 30) heel.

Repeat the last two rounds once more. 28 (35, 42, 49, 56, 63) stitches, 15 (19, 22, 26, 29, 33) instep and 13 (16, 20, 23, 27, 30) heel. Knit one round even.

Foot

Begin to work the instep stitches in *Syncopated Rib Pattern for Instep* from written instructions below while continuing to work the heel stitches in stockinette stitch.

Work until the foot from the tip of the toe to the needles measures approximately 1$\frac{1}{2}$ (1$\frac{3}{4}$, 2, 2$\frac{1}{4}$, 2$\frac{1}{2}$, 2$\frac{3}{4}$)" less than the desired total length.

Syncopated Rib Pattern for Instep,
5", 7" and 9" Sizes only:
(over multiple of 7 stitches + 1 and 1 round)
Round 1: *P1, k1, p1, k2, p1, k1; repeat from * to last stitch, p1.

Syncopated Rib Pattern for Instep,
6", 8" and 10" Sizes only:
(over multiple of 7 stitches + 5 and 1 round)
Round 1: P1, k1, *p1, k1, p1, k2, p1, k1; repeat
from * to last three stitches, p1, k1, p1.

Heel
Hold Stitches for Heel
Work across instep stitches in pattern. With
waste yarn, knit across heel stitches. Drop
waste yarn and go back to start of heel. Knit
across heel stitches with working yarn.

Leg
Continuing in the round, work both instep
and heel stitches in *Syncopated Rib Pattern
for Leg* from written instructions below until
leg measures approximately 4 (4^1/$_2$, 5, 6, 7,
7^1/$_2$)" from waste yarn holding heel stitches.

Bind off all stitches using your favorite toe-up
method. (I used the yarn over bind-off.)

Syncopated Rib Pattern for Leg,
5", 7" and 9" Sizes only:
(over multiple of 7 stitches and 1 round)
Round 1: *P1, k1, p1, k2, p1, k1; repeat
from * to last instep stitch, p1; *k1, p1, k2,
p1, k1, p1; repeat from * to last six heel
stitches, k1, p1, k2, p1, k1.

Syncopated Rib Pattern for Leg,
6", 8" and 10" Sizes only:
(over multiple of 7 stitches and 1 round)
Round 1: P1, k1, *p1, k1, p1, k2, p1, k1;
repeat from * to last three instep stitches,
p1, k1, p1; *k2, [p1, k1] twice, p1; repeat
from * to last two heel stitches, k2.

Insert Afterthought Heel
Carefully pick up the stitches held by the
waste yarn, placing the back-of-leg stitches
on one needle and the bottom-of-foot stitches
on another. There will be an extra stitch on
the top (back-of-leg) needle, so pick up a
stitch in the corner of the heel with the other
needle so that there are 14 (17, 21, 24, 28, 31)
stitches on each needle. If working on dpns,
divide each set of stitches over two dpns.

Join yarn to be used for heel at corner of heel
at the point where the bottom-of-foot stitches
and the back-of-leg stitches meet and begin
working in the round on these 28 (34, 42, 48,
56, 62) stitches.

Round 1: Knit.
Round 2: *K1, SSK, knit to three stitches
before corner of heel, k2tog, k1; repeat
from *.

Repeat Rounds 1 & 2 until 8 (10, 10, 12, 16, 18)
stitches remain. Graft the heel closed from
corner to corner using Kitchener stitch.

Old-School Knee-Highs

Fitting the upper leg portion of knee-highs can be tricky, but knitting from the toe-up allows you to try on and fit as you go. This fun pattern knits up quickly in dk-weight yarn and sports retro-style striping on the cuff and toes. Make yourself a pair and I guarantee you'll feel the urge to dust off your roller skates!

Materials:

Approximately 200 (250, 350, 400, 450, 500) yards dk-weight yarn in MC and 50 (75, 100, 150, 175, 200) yards in CC

Samples use Lorna's Laces Green Line DK (100% organic merino wool) in Mirth (MC on child's socks, CC on women's socks) and Echo (MC on women's socks, CC on child's socks).

US2 (2.75mm) needles or size needed to obtain gauge

Gauge:

$6^1/_2$ stitches/9 rounds per inch in stockinette stitch
12 stitches/9 rounds per inch in unstretched k2, p2 rib

Sizes:

Foot circumference = approximately 5 (6, 7, 8, 9, 10)"

Toe

Using your favorite toe-up method and leaving a 16" tail, cast on three instep stitches and three heel stitches with CC. Knit each stitch with both the working yarn and the tail, ending with 12 loops on the needles (each tail loop is counted as its own stitch). Divide these 12 stitches over your selected needles and place a marker at the start of the instep stitches to indicate the beginning of the round.

If you are substituting a toe, you will need to figure out how many rounds your toe will use and place the MC stripe eight rounds before the final toe round and the CC stripe four rounds before the final toe round.

Round 1 *(and all odd-numbered rounds, except as noted)*: Knit.

Round 2: *K-fb, k2; repeat from * to end of round. 16 stitches.

Round 4: *K-fb, k3; repeat from * to end of round. 20 stitches.

Round 6: *K-fb, k4; repeat from * to end of round. 24 stitches.

Round 7 *(5" size only)*: Switch to MC before knitting, do not break CC.

Round 8: *K-fb, k5; repeat from * to end of round. 28 stitches.

Round 10: *K-fb, k6; repeat from * to end of round. 32 stitches.

Round 11 *(5" size only)*: Switch to CC before knitting, do not break MC.

Round 11 *(6" size only)*: Switch to MC before knitting, do not break CC.

Round 12: *K-fb, k7; repeat from * to end of round. 36 stitches.

Round 14: *K-fb, k8; repeat from * to end of round. 40 stitches.

Round 15 *(5" size only)*: Switch to MC, break CC before knitting.

Round 15 *(6" size only)*: Switch to CC before knitting, do not break MC.

Round 15 *(7" size only)*: Switch to MC before knitting, do not break CC.

6", 7", 8", 9" and 10" Sizes only

Round 16: *K-fb, k9; repeat from * to end of round. 44 stitches.

Round 18: *K-fb, k10; repeat from * to end of round. 48 stitches.

Round 19 *(6" size only)*: Switch to MC, break CC before knitting.

Round 19 *(7" size only)*: Switch to CC before knitting, do not break MC.

Round 19 *(8" size only)*: Switch to MC before knitting, do not break CC.

7", 8", 9" and 10" Sizes only

Round 20: *K-fb, k11; repeat from * to end of round. 52 stitches.

Round 22: *K-fb, k12; repeat from * to end of round. 56 stitches.

Round 23 *(7" size only)*: Switch to MC, break CC before knitting.

Round 23 *(8" size only)*: Switch to CC before knitting, do not break MC.

Round 23 *(9" size only)*: Switch to MC before knitting, do not break CC.

8", 9" and 10" Sizes only

Round 24: *K-fb, k13; repeat from * to end of round. 60 stitches.

Round 26: *K-fb, k14; repeat from * to end of round. 64 stitches.

Round 27 *(8" size only)*: Switch to MC, break CC before knitting.

Round 27 *(9" size only):* Switch to CC before knitting, do not break MC.

Round 27 *(10" size only):* Switch to MC before knitting, do not break CC.

9" and 10" Sizes only

Round 28: *K-fb, k15; repeat from * to end of round. 68 stitches.

Round 30: *K-fb, k16; repeat from * to end of round. 72 stitches.

Round 31 *(9" size only):* Switch to MC, break CC before knitting.

Round 31 *(10" size only):* Switch to CC before knitting, do not break MC.

10" Size only

Round 32: *K-fb, k17; repeat from * to end of round. 76 stitches.

Round 34: *K-fb, k18; repeat from * to end of round. 80 stitches.

Round 35: Switch to MC, break CC before knitting.

Foot

5", 6", 7" and 9" Sizes only

There are now 40 (48, 56, 64) stitches on the needles. Begin working rib pattern for instep as follows: P1, *k2, p2; repeat from * to last three instep stitches, k2, p1; knit across heel stitches.

Work until the foot from the tip of the toe to the needles measures approximately 1$\frac{1}{2}$ (2, 2$\frac{1}{2}$, 3)" less than desired total length.

8" and 10" Sizes only

There are now 72 (80) stitches on the needles. Adjust stitches so that there are 30 (38) instep stitches and 34 (42) heel stitches by moving one stitch from each edge of the instep to the heel. Begin working rib pattern for instep as follows: *P2, k2; repeat from * to last two instep stitches, p2; knit across heel stitches.

Work until the foot from the tip of the toe to the needles measures approximately 3$\frac{1}{2}$ (3$\frac{3}{4}$)" less than the desired total length.

Heel

Hold Stitches for Heel

Work across instep stitches in pattern. With waste yarn, knit across heel stitches. Drop waste yarn and go back to start of heel. Knit across heel stitches with working yarn.

Leg

To get a custom-fitted calf shape, measure the circumference of the sock recipient's calf at the widest point. Then, use *Table 1* to determine the optimal number of calf stitches.

For toddlers and children, it's unlikely that you'll need to increase at all and can just knit the leg as a straight tube using the ribbing's natural stretch to fit their relatively straight leg.

The calculations in *Table 1* for the adult sizes use approximately 30% negative ease which I've found to be the number that strikes a reasonable balance between a sock leg that's too tight and one that's constantly falling down. Note that to maintain the rib pattern, increases must be in multiples of eight.

The increase section of the leg should cover approximately the center ⅓. Determine the desired finished length of the leg by measuring from the crease at the back of the knee to the bottom of the ankle bone. Unless your leg is very straight, you will want to add ½" to 1" to accommodate the stretch of the fabric over the calf.

Determine where to start the increases using the figures in *Table 2*. If your calf height falls outside this table, divide it by three to determine your starting height. If you have a very wide, short leg, you will need to start your increases an inch or two sooner to fit them all in before the stripe section, but this will only be an issue if your measurements fall at the opposite ends of the two tables.

Table 1:

Calf Circumference:	10"	12"	14"	16"	18"	20"	22"	24"
7" Size # of increases:	0	0	8	16	24	32	40	48
8" Size # of increases:	0	0	0	8	16	24	32	40
9" Size # of increases:	0	0	0	0	8	16	24	32
10" Size # of increases:	0	0	0	0	0	8	16	24

Table 2:

Calf Height:	12"	13"	14"	15"	16"	17"	18"	19"
Start Increases At:	4"	4¼"	4¾"	5"	5¼"	5¾"	6"	6¼"
# of Rows in Section:	36	38	43	45	47	52	54	56

Work *Rib Pattern for Leg* as follows over all stitches until leg measures the correct "start increases at" length from the waste yarn placed for heel. For 5" and 6" sizes, work rib until leg measures approximately $3\frac{1}{2}$" less than desired finished length, then skip to Stripe Section.

Rib Pattern for Leg - 5", 6", 7" and 9" Sizes only:
Round 1: P1, *k2, p2; repeat from * to last three stitches of round, k2, p1.

Rib Pattern for Leg - 8" and 10" Sizes only:
Round 1: *P2, k2; repeat from * to end of round.

Increase Section - 7", 8", 9" and 10" Sizes only:
Work a round in pattern, placing a stitch marker after the 14th (17th, 18th, 21st) heel stitch to mark the center back of the leg.
If working 8 to 24 increases, work three rounds even in pattern as established between each increase round.
If working 32 to 48 increases, work one round even in pattern as established between each increase round.

Increase Round 1: Work across instep stitches in pattern; work across heel stitches in pattern to stitch before marker, m1, k1 || k1, m1, work to end of round. Two stitches increased.

Work one to three rounds even in rib (based on the number of increases you're working), knitting the newly increased stitches.

Increase Round 2: Work across instep stitches in pattern; work across heel stitches in pattern to stitch before marker, m1, k1 || k1, m1, work to end of round. Two stitches increased.

Work one to three rounds even in rib, knitting the newly increased stitches.

Increase Round 3: Work across instep stitches in pattern; work across heel stitches in pattern to stitch before marker, m1-pwise, k1 || k1, m1-pwise, work to end of round. Two stitches increased.
Work one to three rounds even in rib, purling the newly increased stitches.

Increase Round 4: Work across instep stitches in pattern; work across heel stitches in pattern to stitch before marker, m1-pwise, k1 || k1, m1-pwise, work to end of round. Two stitches increased.
Work one to three rounds even in rib, purling the newly increased stitches.

Repeat Increase Rounds 1 - 4 (plus accompanying even rounds) until the correct number of stitches needed for your size has been increased. If needed, work even in rib pattern until leg measures 5" less than desired finished length. Do not remove marker at center back of leg.

Stripe Section - All Sizes
Join CC. You will note that the instructions have you knit one round at each color change. This helps to avoid the color "blips" that occur when purling with a new color. Knit only the very first round with the new color, then go back to k2, p2 rib as established in the previous rounds.

5" and 6" Sizes only
Round 1: With CC (do not break MC), knit one round.
Rounds 2 - 6: Work in rib as established using CC.

Round 7: With MC (do not break CC), knit one round.

Rounds 8 - 10: Work in rib as established using MC.

Repeat Rounds 1 - 10 once more, then work Rounds 1 - 6. Break CC and knit one round even with MC. Work in rib as established until sock measures desired finished length, then bind off all stitches using your favorite toe-up method. (I used the yarn over bind-off.)

7", 8", 9" and 10" Sizes only

Round 1: With CC (do not break MC), knit one round.

Rounds 2 - 8: Work in rib as established using CC.

Round 9: With MC (do not break CC), knit one round.

Rounds 10 - 12: Work in rib as established using MC.

Repeat Rounds 1 - 12 once more, then work Rounds 1 - 6. Break CC and knit one round even with MC.

Decrease Round 1: Work instep stitches in rib as established; work heel stitches in rib as established to two stitches before marker, k2tog ‖ SSK, work in rib to end of round.

Round 2: Work even in rib as established.

Repeat the last two rounds an additional three times, decreasing a total of eight stitches. Work in rib as established until sock measures desired finished length, then bind off all stitches using your favorite toe-up method. (I used the yarn over bind-off.)

Insert Afterthought Heel

Carefully pick up the stitches held by the waste yarn, placing the back-of-leg stitches on one needle and the bottom-of-foot stitches on another. There will be an extra stitch on the top (back-of-leg) needle, so pick up a stitch in the corner of the heel with the other needle so there are 21 (25, 29, 35, 37, 43) stitches on each needle. If working on dpns, divide each set of stitches over two dpns.

Join CC at corner of heel at the point where the bottom-of-foot stitches and the back-of-leg stitches meet and begin working in the round on these 42 (50, 58, 70, 74, 86) stitches.

Round 1: *K19 (23, 27, 33, 35, 41), k2tog; repeat from *. 40 (48, 56, 68, 72, 84) stitches.

Round 2: [K8 (10, 12, 15, 16, 19), k2tog] four times. 36 (44, 52, 64, 68, 80) stitches.

Round 3: Knit.

Round 4: [K7 (9, 11, 14, 15, 18), k2tog] four times. 32 (40, 48, 60, 64, 76) stitches.

Round 5: Join MC. Drop but do not break CC. Knit.

Round 6: [K6 (8, 10, 13, 14, 17), k2tog] four times. 28 (36, 44, 56, 60, 72) stitches.

Round 7: Knit.

Round 8: [K5 (7, 9, 12, 13, 16), k2tog] four times. 24 (32, 40, 52, 56, 68) stitches.

Round 9: Break MC. With CC, knit.

Round 10: [K4 (6, 8, 11, 12, 15), k2tog] four times. 20 (28, 36, 48, 52, 64) stitches.

Round 11 *(and all odd-numbered rounds)***:** Knit.

Round 12: [K3 (5, 7, 10, 11, 14), k2tog] four times. 16 (24, 32, 44, 48, 60) stitches.

Continue to decrease in this manner, working one less knit stitch between each k2tog every other round, until 8 (12, 16, 20, 20, 24) stitches remain. Graft heel closed from corner to corner using Kitchener stitch.

Gull Wing

I designed these socks to make the most out of variegated yarn by using a combination of slipped stitches that stretch across multiple rows, and bands of purl stitches that highlight the color changes without being too distracting. The resulting pattern looks like ripples of water flowing across a rough-surfaced rock or the wings of a gull soaring across the sky.

Materials:

Approximately 200 (300, 400) yards fingering-weight yarn

Samples use Lorna's Laces Shepherd Sock (80% superwash wool, 20% nylon) in Icehouse for child's socks and Classic Elite Alpaca Sox (60% alpaca, 20% wool, 20% nylon) in Pebbles for men's socks.

US1 (2.25mm) needles or size needed to obtain gauge

Cable needle or locking stitch marker

Gauge:

8 stitches/11 rounds per inch in stockinette stitch
$10^{1}/_{2}$ stitches/$11^{1}/_{2}$ rounds per inch in wing stitch

Sizes:

Foot circumference = approximately 6 ($7^{1}/_{2}$, 9)"

Toe

Using your favorite toe-up method, cast on 6 (8, 10) instep stitches and 6 (8, 10) heel stitches, dividing them across your selected needles. Place a marker at the start of the instep stitches to indicate the beginning of the round.

Round 1: K-fb, knit to last two instep stitches, k-fb, k1; repeat across heel stitches. 16 (20, 24) stitches.

Round 2: Knit.

Repeat Rounds 1 & 2 an additional 8 (10, 12) times. 48 (60, 72) stitches.

Foot

Begin working the instep stitches in *Wing Stitch* from chart or written instructions below while continuing to work the heel stitches in stockinette stitch. Work until the foot from the tip of the toe to the needles measures approximately 4 (4^3/$_4$, 5^1/$_2$)" less than the desired total length, ending with Round 6 of *Wing Stitch*.

6	5	4	3	2	1	
•	•	•	•	•	•	6
⌐	⌐	—	—	⌐	⌐	5
		V	V			4
		V	V			3
		I	I	I	I	2
		Ⅴ	Ⅴ			1

- ☐ knit
- ⊡ purl
- Ⅴ k1 wrapping yarn around ndl twice
- Ⅱ sl1 with yarn in back, dropping extra wrap
- V sl1 with yarn in back
- ⌐⌐⌐ C3B - sl2 to cable needle and hold in back, k1, k2 from cable needle
- ⌐⌐⌐ C3F - sl1 to cable needle and hold in front, k2, k1 from cable needle

Wing Stitch:

(over 6 stitches and 6 rounds)

Round 1: *K2, [k1 wrapping yarn twice around needle] twice, k2; repeat from *.

Round 2: *K2, [sl1 with yarn in back, dropping extra wrap] twice, k2; repeat from *.

Rounds 3 & 4: *K2, sl2 with yarn in back, k2; repeat from *.

Round 5: *C3B, C3F; repeat from *.

Round 6: Purl.

Heel

Gusset

Round 1: Work instep stitches in *Wing Stitch* as established; k-fb in first heel stitch, knit to last two heel stitches, k-fb, k1.

Round 2: Continue working instep stitches in pattern; knit across all heel stitches.

Repeat Rounds 1 & 2 an additional 13 (15, 17) times. 52 (62, 72) heel stitches.

Turn Heel

Work across instep stitches in pattern. The heel turn will be worked back and forth over the 52 (62, 72) heel stitches.

Row 1 (RS): K37 (45, 53), W&T.

Row 2: P22 (28, 34), W&T.

Row 3: Knit to stitch before wrapped stitch (do not knit any wrapped stitches), W&T.

Row 4: Purl to stitch before wrapped stitch (do not purl any wrapped stitches), W&T.

Repeat Rows 3 & 4 an additional 6 (8, 10) times - there are now 8 (10, 12) wrapped stitches on either side of 8 (10, 12) unwrapped center stitches. Knit to end of heel stitches, lifting wraps RS as they are encountered, then work across instep stitches in pattern.

Heel Flap

Work the heel flap back and forth.

Row 1 (RS): K37 (45, 53), lifting remaining wraps RS, SSK, turn.

Row 2: [Sl1, p1] 11 (14, 17) times, sl1, p2tog, turn.

Row 3: Sl1, k22 (28, 34), SSK, turn.

Repeat Rows 2 & 3 an additional 12 (14, 16) times. Do not turn after working final repeat of Row 3 (one gusset stitch remains on right-hand edge of heel).

Next Round *(6" size only):* Work across instep stitches in pattern; k2tog, k3, [m1, k4] five times, m1. 54 stitches.

Next Round *(7¹/₂" size only):* Work across instep stitches in pattern; k2tog, k1, [m1, k3, m1, k2] five times, m1, k3, m1. 72 stitches.

Next Round *(9" size only):* Work across instep stitches in pattern; k2tog, k2, [m1, k3] 11 times, m1. 84 stitches.

Leg

Continuing in the round, work both instep and heel stitches in *Wing Stitch* (work heel stitches in stockinette stitch if working Rounds 2, 3 or 4 of pattern on instep) until cuff measures approximately 3 (4, 5)" from top of heel flap or 1" less than desired finished length, ending with Round 5 of *Wing Stitch*.

Cuff

Round 1 *(6 " size only):* Purl across instep stitches; [p3, p2tog] six times across heel stitches. 48 stitches.

Round 1 *(7¹/₂" size only):* Purl across instep stitches; [p1, p2tog, p2, p2tog] six times across heel stitches. 60 stitches.

Round 1 *(9" size only):* Purl across instep stitches; [p2, p2tog] 12 times across heel stitches. 72 stitches.

Round 2 *(all sizes):* *K1, p1; repeat from * to end of round.

Repeat Round 2 until ribbing measures 1". Bind off all stitches using your favorite toe-up method. (I used the sewn bind-off.)

——— ❖ ❖ ❖ ———

Toe-Up!

Sydney

Named after my daughter, these ruffled anklets fit her girly, pink-loving personality perfectly. I couldn't resist making another pair for myself out of a wool-free yarn perfect for summer wear. This is a quick, fun project that works well with variegated sock yarn and is totally adorable in any size!

Materials:

Approximately 150 (200, 300, 400, 425, 450) yards of fingering-weight yarn

Samples use SWTC Tofutsies (50% superwash wool, 25% Soysilk, 22$\frac{1}{2}$ % cotton, 2$\frac{1}{2}$ % chitin) in color #731 - Ten Foot Tall for child's socks and Crystal Palace Maizy (82% corn fiber, 18% elastic) in color #1008 - Springtime for women's socks.

US0 (2mm) needles or size needed to obtain gauge

Gauge:

10 stitches/14 rounds per inch in stockinette stitch

Sizes:

Foot circumference = approximately 4 (5, 6, 7, 8, 9)"

Toe

Using your favorite toe-up method and leaving a 16" tail, cast on three instep stitches and three heel stitches. Knit each stitch with both the working yarn and the tail, ending with 12 loops on the needles (each tail loop is counted as its own stitch). Divide these 12 stitches over your selected needles and place a marker at the start of the instep stitches to indicate the beginning of the round.

Round 1: *K3, place marker; repeat from * to end of round.

Round 2: *K-fb, knit to next marker; repeat from * to end of round. 16 stitches.

Round 3: Knit.

Repeat Rounds 2-3 an additional 6 (8, 10, 14, 16, 18) times. 40 (48, 56, 72, 80, 88) stitches.

Foot

There are now 40 (48, 56, 72, 80, 88) stitches on the needles. Begin working the instep stitches in *Eyelet Rib* from the written instructions below while continuing to work the heel stitches in stockinette stitch. Work until the foot from the tip of the toe to the needles measures approximately 1 (1, $1^1/_2$, $1^1/_2$, $1^3/_4$, 2)" less than the desired total length, ending with Round 3 of pattern.

Eyelet Rib:

(over multiple of 4 stitches and 4 rounds)

Round 1: P1, *k2, p2; repeat from * to last three stitches, k2, p1.

Round 2: P1, *k2tog, YO, p2; repeat from * to last three stitches, k2tog, YO, p1.

Round 3: Repeat Round 1.

Round 4: P1, *YO, SSK, p2; repeat from * to last three stitches, YO, SSK, p1.

Heel

Work across instep stitches in Round 4 of pattern. The heel will be worked back and forth on the 20 (24, 28, 36, 40, 44) heel stitches.

Shape Bottom of Heel

Row 1 (RS): Knit to last stitch on needle, W&T.

Row 2: Purl to last stitch on needle, W&T.

Row 3: Knit to stitch before wrapped stitch (do not knit across any wrapped stitches), W&T.

Row 4: Purl to stitch before wrapped stitch (do not purl across any wrapped stitches), W&T.

Repeat Rows 3 & 4 an additional 5 (6, 8, 10, 12, 13) times - there are now 7 (8, 10, 12, 14, 15) wrapped stitches on either side of 6 (8, 8, 12, 12, 14) unwrapped center stitches.

Shape Top of Heel

Row 1 (RS): Knit to first wrapped stitch (do not knit across any wrapped stitches), lift wrap RS, turn.

Row 2 (WS): Sl1, purl to first wrapped stitch (do not purl across any wrapped stitches), lift wrap WS, turn.

Row 3: Sl1, knit to next wrapped stitch (just past the stitch unwrapped on the previous RS row), lift wrap RS, turn.

Row 4: Sl1, purl to next wrapped stitch (just past the stitch unwrapped on the previous WS row), lift wrap WS, turn.

Repeat Rows 3 & 4 an additional 4 (5, 7, 9, 11, 12) times - a single wrapped stitch remains on either side of heel.

Next Row: Sl1, knit to last wrapped stitch, lift wrap RS, but do not turn. You should be at the beginning of the instep stitches.

Next Round: Work instep stitches in pattern as established; lift wrap RS, knit to end of heel stitches.

Leg

Continuing in the round, work *Eyelet Rib* across all stitches for $1\frac{1}{2}$ (2, 2, 2, 2, $2\frac{1}{2}$)" from top of heel.

Cuff

Round 1 *(4" size only):* *[K1, p1] three times, k2tog, p1; repeat from * an additional three times, [k1, p1] twice. 36 stitches.

Round 1 *(5" size only):* *K1, p1; repeat from * to end of round. 48 stitches.

Round 1 *(6" size only):* *[K1, p1] twice, k2tog, p1; repeat from * an additional seven times. 48 stitches.

Round 1 *(7" size only):* *K1, p1; repeat from * to end of round. 72 stitches.

Round 1 *(8" size only):* *[K1, p1] three times, k2tog, p1; repeat from * an additional seven times, [k1, p1] four times. 72 stitches.

Round 1 *(9" size only):* *[K1, p1] nine times, k2tog, p1; repeat from * an additional three times, [k1, p1] twice. 84 stitches.

Round 2 *(all sizes):* *K1, p1; repeat from * to end of round.

Repeat Round 2 for $\frac{1}{2}$", then knit one round. Turn sock inside out - the rest of the ruffle will be worked with the wrong side of the sock facing you and in the opposite direction of the body of the sock.

Ruffle

Round 1: Sl1, k3, p2, *k4, p2; repeat from * to end of round.

Rounds 2 - 6: *K4, p2; repeat from * to end of round.

Round 7: *K2, YO, k2, p2; repeat from * to end of round. 42 (56, 56, 84, 84, 98) stitches.

Round 8: *K5, p2; repeat from * to end of round.

Round 9: *K2, YO, k1, YO, k2, p2; repeat from * to end of round. 54 (72, 72, 108, 108, 126) stitches.

Round 10: *K7, p2; repeat from * to end of round.

Round 11: *K2, YO, k3, YO, k2, p2; repeat from * to end of round. 66 (88, 88, 132, 132, 154) stitches.

Round 12: *K9, p2; repeat from * to end of round.

Round 13: *K2, YO, k5, YO, k2, p2; repeat from * to end of round. 78 (104, 104, 156, 156, 182) stitches.

Round 14: *K11, p2; repeat from * to end of round.

Round 15: *K2, YO, k7, YO, k2, p2; repeat from * to end of round. 90 (120, 120, 180, 180, 210) stitches.

Round 16: *K13, p2; repeat from * to end of round.

Round 17: *K2, YO, k9, YO, k2, p2; repeat from * to end of round. 102 (136, 136, 204, 204, 238) stitches.

Round 18: *K15, p2; repeat from * to end of round.

5", 6", 7", 8" and 9" Sizes only

Round 19: *K2, YO, k11, YO, k2, p2; repeat from * to end of round. - (152, 152, 228, 228, 266) stitches.

Round 20: *K17, p2; repeat from * to end of round.

6", 7", 8" and 9" Sizes only

Round 21: *K2, YO, k13, YO, k2, p2; repeat from * to end of round. - (-, 168, 252, 252, 294) stitches.

Round 22: *K19, p2; repeat from * to end of round.

7", 8" and 9" Sizes only

Round 23: *K2, YO, k15, YO, k2, p2; repeat from * to end of round. - (-, -, 276, 276, 322) stitches.

Round 24: *K21, p2; repeat from * to end of round.

All Sizes

Next Round: Purl all stitches.

Next Round: *K1, YO; repeat from * to end of round.

Bind off all stitches using your favorite toe-up method. (I used the p2tog bind-off.)

Toe-Up!

Fjordland

From the day I first saw the amazing textured color patterns of the Bohuslan Collective of Sweden, I was entranced. Simple color repeats that utilize both knit and purl stitches give color patterns a glowing, beaded quality while being surprisingly easy to work. This sock is a nod to my Scandinavian roots and my passion for the incredible knitting styles that originated in that part of the world.

Materials:

Approximately 75 (125, 175, 200, 225, 250) yards of fingering-weight yarn in MC, 75 (125, 175, 200, 225, 250) yards in CC1 and 75 (125, 175, 200, 225, 250) yards in CC2

Samples use Dale of Norway Baby Ull (100% merino wool) in 9436 for MC, 3871 for CC1 and 9436 for CC2 for child's socks and Cascade Heritage (75% superwash merino, 25% nylon) in 5605 for MC, 5614 for CC1 and 5618 for CC2 for women's socks.

US0 (2mm) needles or size needed to obtain gauge

Gauge:

9 stitches/12 rows per inch in stockinette stitch

Sizes:

Foot circumference = approximately 4 (5, 6, 7, 8, 9)"

Toe

Using your favorite toe-up method and leaving a 16" tail, cast on three heel stitches and three instep stitches with MC (unlike the other patterns in this book, the heel stitches for these socks will be worked first followed by the instep stitches). Knit each stitch with both the working yarn and the tail, ending with 12 loops on the needles (each tail loop is counted as its own stitch). Divide these twelve stitches over your selected needles and place a marker at the start of the heel stitches to indicate the beginning of the round.

Round 1 (*and all odd-numbered rounds*)**:** Knit.

Round 2: *K-fb, k2; repeat from * to end of round. 16 stitches.

Round 4: *K-fb, k3; repeat from * to end of round. 20 stitches.

Round 6: *K-fb, k4; repeat from * to end of round. 24 stitches.

Round 8: *K-fb, k5; repeat from * to end of round. 28 stitches.

Round 10: *K-fb, k6; repeat from * to end of round. 32 stitches.

Round 12: *K-fb, k7; repeat from * to end of round. 36 stitches.

5", 6", 7", 8" and 9" Sizes only

Round 14: *K-fb, k8; repeat from * to end of round. 40 stitches.

Round 16: *K-fb, k9; repeat from * to end of round. 44 stitches.

6", 7", 8" and 9" Sizes only

Round 18: *K-fb, k10; repeat from * to end of round. 48 stitches.

Round 20: *K-fb, k11; repeat from * to end of round. 52 stitches.

Round 22: *K-fb, k12; repeat from * to end of round. 56 stitches.

7", 8" and 9" Sizes only

Round 24: *K-fb, k13; repeat from * to end of round. 60 stitches.

Round 26: *K-fb, k14; repeat from * to end of round. 64 stitches.

8" and 9" Sizes only

Round 28: *K-fb, k15; repeat from * to end of round. 68 stitches.

Round 30: *K-fb, k16; repeat from * to end of round. 72 stitches.

9" Size only

Round 32: *K-fb, k17; repeat from * to end of round. 76 stitches.

Round 34: *K-fb, k18; repeat from * to end of round. 80 stitches.

Foot

There are now 36 (44, 56, 64, 72, 80) stitches on the needles. Begin working all stitches according to the color chart below. Work until the foot from the tip of the toe to the needles measures approximately 1 (1, 1 1/2, 1 1/2, 1 3/4, 2)" less than the desired total length, ending, if possible, with a single-color round of the color pattern.

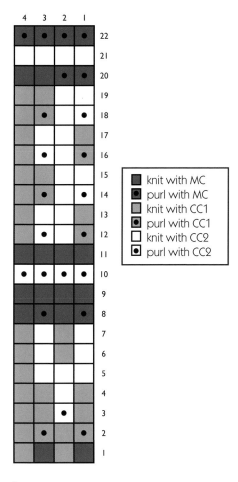

Shape Bottom of Heel

Row 1 (RS): Knit to last stitch on needle, W&T.

Row 2: Purl to last stitch on needle, W&T.

Row 3: Knit to stitch before wrapped stitch (do not knit across any wrapped stitches), W&T.

Row 4: Purl to stitch before wrapped stitch (do not purl across any wrapped stitches), W&T.

Repeat Rows 3 & 4 an additional 4 (5, 7, 9, 10, 11) times - there are now 6 (7, 9, 11, 12, 13) wrapped stitches on either side of 6 (8, 10, 10, 12, 14) unwrapped center stitches.

Shape Top of Heel

Row 1 (RS): Knit to first wrapped stitch (do not knit across any wrapped stitches), lift wrap RS, turn.

Row 2 (WS): Sl1, purl to first wrapped stitch (do not purl across any wrapped stitches), lift wrap WS, turn.

Row 3: Sl1, knit to next wrapped stitch (just past the stitch unwrapped on the previous RS row), lift wrap RS, turn.

Row 4: Sl1, purl to next wrapped stitch (just past the stitch unwrapped on the previous WS row), lift wrap WS, turn.

Repeat Rows 3 & 4 an additional 4 (5, 7, 9, 10, 11) times - all wraps have been lifted. You are at the beginning of the heel stitches with the RS facing, ready to begin the leg.

Heel

The heel will be worked back and forth on the 18 (22, 28, 32, 36, 40) heel stitches with MC only (do not cut the other colors, just drop them while the heel is worked).

Leg

Continuing in the round, work the color pattern as established across all stitches until leg measures approximately $1\frac{1}{2}$ (2, $3\frac{1}{2}$, 5, 6, 6)" from top of heel or 1" less than desired finished length.

Cuff

Break CC1 and CC2. With MC, work k1, p1 rib for 1". Bind off all stitches using your favorite toe-up method. (I used the sewn bind-off.)

❖ ❖ ❖

Fancy Socks

Diamond Lucy

A subtly textured diamond pattern and a high-relief seeded rib wrap around the leg of these mirror-image socks. I chose the yarn for this design very carefully to ensure that the stitch pattern would not disappear into a deeply colored or highly textured fiber. When selecting yarn for your socks, look for a tightly twisted, smooth, light-colored yarn to make the pattern stand out.

Materials:

Approximately 400 yards of fingering-weight yarn

Sample uses Blue Moon Seduction (50% merino wool, 50% Tencel) in Blue Moonstone.

US1 (2.25mm) needles or size needed to obtain gauge

Gauge:

8 stitches/10 rounds per inch in stockinette stitch

Size:

Foot circumference = approximately 8 1/2"

Toe

Using your favorite toe-up method, cast on 31 instep stitches and 31 heel stitches, dividing them over your selected needles. The toe will be worked back and forth across the instep stitches.

Shape Bottom of Toe

Row 1 (RS): K30, W&T.

Row 2 (WS): P29, W&T.

Row 3: Knit to stitch before wrapped stitch (do not knit across any wrapped stitches), W&T.

Row 4: Purl to stitch before wrapped stitch (do not purl across any wrapped stitches), W&T.

Repeat Rows 3 & 4 an additional eight times - there are now 10 wrapped stitches on either side of 11 unwrapped center stitches.

Shape Top of Toe

Row 1 (RS): Knit to first wrapped stitch (do not knit across any wrapped stitches), lift wrap RS, turn.

Row 2 (WS): Sl1, purl to first wrapped stitch (do not purl across any wrapped stitches), lift wrap WS, turn.

Row 3: Sl1, knit to next wrapped stitch (just past the stitch unwrapped on the previous RS row), lift wrap RS, turn.

Row 4: Sl1, purl to next wrapped stitch (just past the stitch unwrapped on the previous WS row), lift wrap WS, turn.

Repeat Rows 3 & 4 an additional seven times - a single wrapped stitch remains on either side of toe.

Next Round: Sl1, k29, lift wrap RS, but do not turn; knit across heel stitches.

Next Round *(Left Sock only):* Lift wrap RS to hide the final wrap (which is at the beginning of the round), k1, [p1, k-tbl] twice, k1, p1, k-tbl, [p2, k2, p1, k2] three times, p1; knit across heel stitches.

Next Round *(Right Sock only):* Lift wrap RS to hide the final wrap (which is at the beginning of the round), but instead of knitting the stitch with its wrap, purl them together, [k2, p1, k2, p2] three times, k-tbl, k1, [p1, k-tbl] twice, k1, p1, k-tbl; knit across heel stitches.

Foot

Begin to work the instep stitches in the *Diamond Texture for Instep* from charts on p. 92 or written instructions on p. 90 while continuing to work the heel stitches in stockinette stitch. Work until the foot from the tip of the toe to the needles measures approximately 5" less than the desired total length.

Diamond Texture for Instep - Left Sock:
(over 31 stitches and 8 rounds)
Round 1: K-tbl, p1, k1, [k-tbl, p1] twice, k1, k-tbl, k1, p2, k3, p2, k2, p3, k2, p2, k3, p2.
Round 2: K-tbl, k1, [p1, k-tbl] twice, k1, p1, k-tbl, [k2, p2, k1, p2] three times, k1.
Round 3: K-tbl, p1, k1, [k-tbl, p1] twice, k1, k-tbl, p1, k2, p3, k2, p2, k3, p2, k2, p3, k2.
Round 4: K-tbl, k1, [p1, k-tbl] twice, k1, p1, k-tbl, [p2, k2, p1, k2] three times, p1.
Round 5: Repeat Round 3.
Round 6: Repeat Round 2.
Round 7: Repeat Round 1.
Round 8: Repeat Round 4.

Diamond Texture for Instep - Right Sock :
(over 31 stitches and 8 rounds)
Round 1: K2, p3, k2, p2, k3, p2, k2, p3, k2, p1, k-tbl, p1, k1, [k-tbl, p1] twice, k1, k-tbl.
Round 2: K1, [p2, k1, p2, k2] three times, k-tbl, k1, [p1, k-tbl] twice, k1, p1, k-tbl.
Round 3: P2, k3, p2, k2, p3, k2, p2, k3, p2, k1, k-tbl, p1, k1, [k-tbl, p1] twice, k1, k-tbl.
Round 4: P1, [k2, p1, k2, p2] three times, k-tbl, k1, [p1, k-tbl] twice, k1, p1, k-tbl.
Round 5: Repeat Round 3.
Round 6: Repeat Round 2.
Round 7: Repeat Round 1.
Round 8: Repeat Round 4.

Heel

Gusset

Round 1: Work instep stitches in *Diamond Texture for Instep* as established; k-fb in first heel stitch, knit to last two heel stitches, k-fb, k1.
Round 2: Continue working instep stitches in pattern; knit across heel stitches.

Repeat Rounds 1 & 2 an additional 15 times.

Turn Heel

Work across instep stitches in pattern. The heel turn will be worked back and forth on the 63 heel stitches.
Row 1 (RS): K46, W&T.
Row 2 (WS): P29, W&T.
Row 3: Knit to stitch before wrapped stitch (do not knit across any wrapped stitches), W&T.
Row 4: Purl to stitch before wrapped stitch (do not purl across any wrapped stitches), W&T.

Repeat Rows 3 & 4 an additional eight times - there are now 10 wrapped stitches on either side of 11 unwrapped center stitches. Knit to end of heel stitches, lifting wraps RS as they are encountered, then work across instep stitches in *Diamond Texture for Instep* as established.

Heel Flap

Work heel flap back and forth.
Row 1 (RS): K46, lifting remaining wraps RS, SSK, turn.
Row 2 (WS): Sl1 with yarn in front, [p1, sl1 with yarn in back] 14 times, p1, p2tog, turn.
Row 3: Sl1, k29, SSK, turn.
Row 4: Sl1 with yarn in front, [sl1 with yarn in back, p1] 14 times, sl1 with yarn in back, p2tog, turn.
Row 5: Repeat Row 3.

Repeat Rows 2 - 5 an additional six times, then work Rows 2 & 3 once more. Do not turn after working final repeat of Row 3 (one gusset stitch remains on right-hand edge of heel).

Next Round *(Left Sock only):* Work across instep stitches in pattern; k2tog, knit to last heel stitch, k-fb. 32 heel stitches.
Next Round *(Right Sock only):* Work across instep stitches in pattern; k2tog-fb, knit to end of heel stitches. 32 heel stitches.

Toe-Up!

Leg

Continuing in the round, work the *Diamond Texture for Instep* as established across instep and work the 32 heel stitches in *Diamond Texture for Back of Leg* from chart on p. 92 or written instructions below, making sure to work the same round on the back of the leg that you just worked on the instep so that the stitch pattern will line up. Work until leg measures approximately 5" from top of heel flap, ending with Round 8 of pattern.

Diamond Texture for Back of Leg - Left Sock:
(over 32 stitches and 8 rounds)

Round 1: K2, p3, k2, p2, k3, p2, k2, p3, k2, p1, k-tbl, p1, k1, [k-tbl, p1] twice, k1, k-tbl, p1.

Round 2: K1, [p2, k1, p2, k2] three times, k-tbl, k1, [p1, k-tbl] twice, k1, p1, k-tbl, p1.

Round 3: P2, k3, p2, k2, p3, k2, p2, k3, p2, k1, k-tbl, p1, k1, [k-tbl, p1] twice, k1, k-tbl, p1.

Round 4: P1, [k2, p1, k2, p2] three times, k-tbl, k1, [p1, k-tbl] twice, k1, p1, k-tbl, p1.

Round 5: Repeat Round 3.

Round 6: Repeat Round 2.

Round 7: Repeat Round 1.

Round 8: Repeat Round 4.

Diamond Texture for Back of Leg - Right Sock:
(over 32 stitches and 8 rounds)

Round 1: P1, k-tbl, k1, [p1, k-tbl] twice, k1, p1, k-tbl, [k2, p2, k1, p2] three times, k1.

Round 2: P1, k-tbl, p1, k1, [k-tbl, p1] twice, k1, k-tbl, p1, k2, p3, k2, p2, k3, p2, k2, p3, k2.

Round 3: P1, k-tbl, k1, [p1, k-tbl] twice, k1, p1, k-tbl, [p2, k2, p1, k2] three times, p1.

Round 4: Repeat Round 2.

Round 5: Repeat Round 1.

Round 6: P1, k-tbl, p1, k1, [k-tbl, p1] twice, k1, k-tbl, k1, p2, k3, p2, k2, p3, k2, p2, k3, p2.

Round 7: Repeat Round 3.

Round 8 (all but final round of leg): Repeat Round 6.

Round 8 (final round of leg only): P1, k-tbl, p1, k1, [k-tbl, p1] twice, k1, [k-tbl, p1] 11 times, k-tbl.

Cuff

Left Sock

Round 1: K-tbl, p1, k1, [k-tbl, p1] twice, k1, [k-tbl, p1] 11 times, k-tbl; [k-tbl, p1] 12 times, k1, [k-tbl, p1] twice, k1, k-tbl, p1.

Round 2: K-tbl, k1, [p1, k-tbl] twice, k1, [p1, k-tbl] 12 times; [k-tbl, p1] 11 times, k-tbl, k1, [p1, k-tbl] twice, k1, p1, k-tbl, p1.

Repeat Rounds 1 & 2 for 1". Bind off all stitches using your preferred method.

Right Sock

Round 1: [K-tbl, p1] 12 times, k1, [k-tbl, p1] twice, k1, k-tbl; p1, k-tbl, p1, k1, [k-tbl, p1] twice, k1, [k-tbl, p1] 11 times, k-tbl.

Round 2: [K-tbl, p1] 11 times, k-tbl, k1, [p1, k-tbl] twice, k1, p1, k-tbl; p1, k-tbl, k1, [p1, k-tbl] twice, k1, [p1, k-tbl] 12 times.

Repeat Rounds 1 & 2 for 1", ending final round after working the instep stitches only. Bind off all stitches using your preferred method.

Diamond Texture for Instep - Left Sock

31	30	29	28	27	26	25	24	23	22	21	20	19	18	17	16	15	14	13	12	11	10	9	8	7	6	5	4	3	2	1	
•		•			•	•			•			•	•			•			•	•	B	•		B	•	B	•			B	8
•	•			•	•			•	•	•			•	•			•	•		•	B		•	B	•	B		•		B	7
	•	•		•	•			•	•		•	•			•	•		•	•		B	•		B	•	B	•			B	6
		•	•	•			•	•			•	•			•	•	•			•	B		•	B	•	B		•	•	B	5
•		•			•		•	•			•		•			•		•	•	•	B	•		B	•	B	•			B	4
		•	•		•	•		•				•	•			•	•	•		•	B		•	B	•	B	•			B	3
	•	•		•	•		•	•			•	•			•	•		•	•		B	•		B	•	B	•	•		B	2
•	•			•	•			•	•			•	•			•	•		•	•	B		•	B	•	B		•		B	1

Diamond Texture for Back of Leg - Left Sock

32	31	30	29	28	27	26	25	24	23	22	21	20	19	18	17	16	15	14	13	12	11	10	9	8	7	6	5	4	3	2	1	
•	B	•		B	•	B	•		B	•	•			•			•	•			•		•	•		•		•		•	•	8
•	B		•	B	•	B		•	B	•			•	•	•			•	•		•	•		•		•	•	•				7
•	B	•		B	•	B	•		B		•	•			•		•	•		•	•		•	•		•	•		•	•		6
•	B		•	B	•	B		•	B		•	•				•	•		•	•	•		•	•			•		•	•		5
•	B		•	B	•	B	•		B	•			•			•	•		•	•		•	•		•		•	•		•	•	4
•	B		•	B	•	B	•		B		•	•		•	•		•	•		•	•		•	•		•	•		•	•		3
•	B	•		B	•	B	•		B		•	•		•	•		•	•		•	•	•		•		•	•		•	•		2
•	B		•	B	•	B		B	•		•	•		•	•		•	•		•	•		•	•		•	•		•	•		1

Diamond Texture for Instep - Right Sock

31	30	29	28	27	26	25	24	23	22	21	20	19	18	17	16	15	14	13	12	11	10	9	8	7	6	5	4	3	2	1	
B	•		B	•	B	•		B	•	•			•			•	•			•		•	•		•				•		8
B	•		B	•	B		•	B	•			•	•	•			•	•		•	•		•		•	•	•				7
B	•		B	•	B			B		•	•			•	•		•	•		•	•		•		•	•		•	•		6
B		•	B	•	B		•	B		•	•				•	•		•	•		•	•		•		•	•		•	5
B	•		B	•	B	•		B	•	•			•			•	•		•	•		•	•		•			•		•	4
B		•	B	•	B		•	B		•	•		•	•		•	•		•	•		•	•			•		•	•		3
B	•		B	•	B	•		B		•	•		•	•		•	•		•	•		•	•		•		•	•		•	2
B		•	B	•	B		B	•		•	•		•	•		•	•		•	•		•	•		•		•	•	•		1

Diamond Texture for Back of Leg - Right Sock

32	31	30	29	28	27	26	25	24	23	22	21	20	19	18	17	16	15	14	13	12	11	10	9	8	7	6	5	4	3	2	1	
•	•				•	•			•	•	•			•	•			•	•		B		•	B	•	B		•		B	•	8
•			•			•			•		•	•		•			•	•		•	B	•		B	•	B	•			B	•	7
•	•				•	•		•	•	•		•	•			•	•		•	•	B			B	•	B	•		•	B	•	6
	•	•		•	•			•	•		•	•			•	•		•	•		B	•		B	•	B	•			B	•	5
		•	•		•	•			•	•		•	•		•	•			•	•	B		•	B	•	B			•	B	•	4
•			•	•		•			•	•		•	•		•	•		•	•	•	B		•	B	•	B	•			B	•	3
		•	•		•	•			•	•		•	•		•	•		•	•		B	•		B	•	B	•			B	•	2
	•	•		•	•			•	•		•	•			•	•		•	•		B	•		B	•	B	•		B	•	1

Legend:

- ☐ knit
- ⊡ purl
- B k-tbl

The Dude Abides

Inspired by the classic Cowichan-style sweater worn by Jeff Lebowski (aka "The Dude") in one of my favorite movies, "The Big Lebowski", these fun colorwork socks could easily be worked in worsted-weight yarn on slightly bigger needles for your own dude.

Materials:

Approximately 250 yards sport-weight yarn in MC and 200 yards in CC

Sample uses Lorna's Laces Shepherd Sport (100% superwash wool) in Chocolate for MC and Mountain Colors Bearfoot (60% superwash wool, 25% mohair, 15% nylon) in Copper for CC.

US2 (2.75mm) needles or size needed to obtain gauge

Gauge:

8 stitches/11 rounds per inch in colorwork pattern

Size:

Foot circumference = approximately 8"

Toe

Using your favorite toe-up method, cast on eight instep stitches and eight heel stitches, dividing them across your selected needles. Place a marker at the start of the instep stitches to indicate the beginning of the round.

Shape Inner Edge of Toe

Round 1: K-fb, knit to last two instep stitches, k-fb, k1; repeat across heel stitches. 20 stitches.

Repeat Round 1 an additional seven times. 48 stitches.

Shape Outer Edge of Right Sock Toe

Round 1: Knit.
Round 2: Knit to last two instep stitches, k-fb, k1; k-fb, knit across remaining heel stitches. 50 stitches.

Repeat Rounds 1 & 2 an additional seven times. 64 stitches. Knit one round even.

Shape Outer Edge of Left Sock Toe

Round 1: Knit.
Round 2: K-fb, knit across remaining instep stitches; knit to last two heel stitches, k-fb, k1. 50 stitches.

Repeat Rounds 1 & 2 an additional seven times. 64 stitches. Knit one round even.

Foot

Work all stitches in color pattern from chart on p. 95 until the foot from the tip of the toe to the needles measures approximately $2\frac{1}{4}$" less than the desired total length.

Heel

Hold Stitches for Heel

Work across instep stitches in pattern. With waste yarn, knit across heel stitches. Drop waste yarn and go back to start of heel.

Work heel stitches in color pattern as established.

Leg

Continuing in the round, work color pattern as established until leg measures approximately 5" from waste yarn holding heel stitches. Cut CC. With MC, work k2, p2 rib for 1". Bind off all stitches using your favorite toe-up method. (I used the yarn over bind-off.)

Insert Afterthought Heel

Carefully pick up the stitches held by the waste yarn, placing the back-of-leg stitches on one needle and the bottom-of-foot stitches on another. There will be an extra stitch on the top (back-of-leg) needle, so pick up a stitch in the corner of the heel with the other needle so that there are 33 stitches on each needle. If working on dpns, divide each set of stitches over two dpns.

Join MC at corner of heel at the point where the bottom-of-foot stitches and the back-of-leg stitches meet and begin working in the round on these 66 stitches.

Round 1: Knit.
Round 2: *K1, SSK, knit to three stitches before corner of heel, k2tog, k1; repeat from *.

Repeat Rounds 1 & 2 until 20 stitches remain, then repeat Round 2 only until 14 stitches remain. Graft the heel closed from corner to corner using Kitchener stitch.

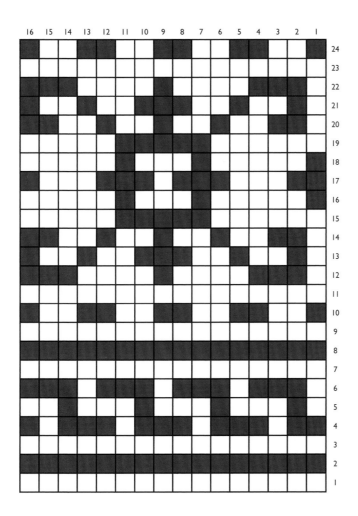

knit with MC
knit with CC

❖ ❖ ❖

The Dude Abides

Candelabra Socks

Orange is one of those colors that people feel very strongly about, and I happen to love it. I couldn't resist this gorgeous skein of Mountain Colors yarn in a brilliant orange hue, and a stitch pattern mimicking candles seemed the ideal choice for this sock. Of course, nothing says that you need to use orange yarn - this pattern would look lovely in any solid or very gently variegated hue.

Materials:

Approximately 400 yards of fingering-weight yarn

Sample uses Mountain Colors Bearfoot (60% wool, 40% mohair) in Marigold.

US1 (2.25mm) needles or size needed to obtain gauge

Cable needle

Gauge:

8 stitches/11 rounds per inch in stockinette stitch

Size:

Foot circumference = approximately 7^1/$_2$"

Toe

Using your favorite toe-up method, cast on 31 instep stitches and 31 heel stitches, dividing them over your selected needles. The toe will be worked back and forth across the instep stitches.

Shape Bottom of Toe

Row 1 (RS): K30, W&T.

Row 2 (WS): P29, W&T.

Row 3: Knit to stitch before wrapped stitch (do not knit across any wrapped stitches), W&T.

Row 4: Purl to stitch before wrapped stitch (do not purl across any wrapped stitches), W&T.

Repeat Rows 3 & 4 an additional 8 times - there are now 10 wrapped stitches on either side of 11 unwrapped center stitches.

Shape Top of Toe

Row 1 (RS): Knit to first wrapped stitch (do not knit across any wrapped stitches), lift wrap RS, turn.

Row 2 (WS): Sl1, purl to first wrapped stitch (do not purl across any wrapped stitches), lift wrap WS, turn.

Row 3: Sl1, knit to next wrapped stitch (just past the stitch unwrapped on the previous RS row), lift wrap RS, turn.

Row 4: Sl1, purl to next wrapped stitch (just past the stitch unwrapped on the previous WS row), lift wrap WS, turn.

Repeat Rows 3 & 4 an additional seven times - a single wrapped stitch remains on either side of toe.

Next Round: Sl1, k29, lift wrap RS, but do not turn; knit across heel stitches.

Next Round: Lift wrap RS to hide the final wrap (which is at the beginning of the round), k4, [m1, k7] three times, m1, k5; knit across heel stitches. 66 stitches, 35 instep and 31 heel.

Foot

Begin to work the instep stitches in the *Candelabra Pattern* from chart on p. 99 or written instructions below while continuing to work the heel stitches in stockinette stitch. Work until the foot from the tip of the toe to the needles measures approximately 4 ³/₄" less than the desired total length.

Candelabra Pattern:

(over 35 stitches and 16 rounds)

Round 1: Sl1, p1, k8, p1, sl1, p4, C3B, p4, sl1, p1, k8, p1, sl1.

Round 2: K1, p1, k8, p1, k1, p4, k3, p4, k1, p1, k8, p1, k1.

Round 3: Sl1, p1, C4B, C4F, p1, sl1, p4, C3B, p4, sl1, p1, C4B, C4F, p1, sl1.

Round 4: Repeat Round 2.

Round 5: Sl1, p1, k2, p4, k2, p1, sl1, p4, C3B, p4, sl1, p1, k2, p4, k2, p1, sl1.

Round 6: K1, p1, k2, p4, k2, p1, k1, p4, k1, C2F, p4, k1, p1, k2, p4, k2, p1, k1.

Round 7: Sl1, p1, C4F, C4B, p1, sl1, p2, C3B, p1, C3F, p2, sl1, p1, C4F, C4B, p1, sl1.

Round 8: K1, p1, k8, p1, k1, p2, [k-tbl, p1] three times, k-tbl, p2, k1, p1, k8, p1, k1.

Round 9: Sl1, p1, k8, p1, sl1, p2, [k-tbl, p1] three times, k-tbl, p2, sl1, p1, k8, p1, sl1.

Round 10: Repeat Round 8.

Round 11: Sl1, p1, C4B, C4F, p1, sl1, p2, [k-tbl, p1] three times, k-tbl, p2, sl1, p1, C4B, C4F, p1, sl1.

Round 12: Repeat Round 8.

Round 13: Sl1, p1, k2, p4, k2, p1, sl1, p1, T2B-tbl, p1, [k-tbl, p1] twice, T2F-tbl, p1, sl1, p1, k2, p4, k2, p1, sl1.

Round 14: K1, p1, k2, p4, k2, p1, k1, [p1, k-tbl, p2, k-tbl] twice, p1, k1, p1, k2, p4, k2, p1, k1.

Round 15: Sl1, p1, C4F, C4B, p1, sl1, p3, T2B-tbl, p1, T2F-tbl, p3, sl1, p1, C4F, C4B, p1, sl1.

Round 16: K1, p1, k8, p1, k1, p3, [k-tbl, p3] twice, k1, p1, k8, p1, k1.

Heel

Gusset

Round 1: Work instep stitches in *Candelabra Pattern* as established; k-fb in first heel stitch, knit to last 2 heel stitches, k-fb, k1.

Round 2: Continue working instep stitches in pattern; knit across heel stitches.

Repeat Rounds 1 & 2 an additional 15 times.

Turn Heel

Work across instep stitches in pattern. The heel turn will be worked back and forth on the 63 heel stitches.

Row 1 (RS): K46, W&T.

Row 2 (WS): P29, W&T.

Row 3: Knit to stitch before wrapped stitch (do not knit across any wrapped stitches), W&T.

Row 4: Purl to stitch before wrapped stitch (do not purl across any wrapped stitches), W&T.

Repeat Rows 3 & 4 an additional 8 times - there are now 10 wrapped stitches on either side of 11 unwrapped center stitches. Knit to end of heel stitches, lifting wraps RS as they are encountered, then work across instep stitches in pattern.

Heel Flap

Work heel flap back and forth.

Row 1 (RS): K46, lifting remaining wraps RS, SSK, turn.

Row 2 (WS): Sl1, [p1, k1] 14 times, p1, SSK, turn.

Row 3: Sl1, [k1, p1, sl1, p1] seven times, k1, p2tog, turn.

Repeat Rows 2 & 3 an additional 14 times. Do not turn after working final repeat of Row 3 (one gusset stitch remains on right-hand edge of heel).

Next Round: Work across instep stitches in pattern; p2tog, [k1, p1] 15 times. 31 heel stitches.

Leg

Continuing in the round, work the *Candelabra Pattern* as established across instep and work the 31 heel stitches in alternating slipped rib as follows:

Round 1: [P1, k1, p1, sl1] seven times, p1, k1, p1.

Round 2: [P1, k1] 15 times, p1.

Work until leg measures approximately 5" from top of heel flap, ending with Round 16 of *Candelabra Pattern*.

Toe-Up!

Candelabra Pattern Chart

35	34	33	32	31	30	29	28	27	26	25	24	23	22	21	20	19	18	17	16	15	14	13	12	11	10	9	8	7	6	5	4	3	2	1	

(35-stitch by 16-row cable and lace chart; symbols as given in the key below)

Key

- ☐ knit
- ⦁ purl
- V sl1 purlwise with yarn in back
- B k-tbl
- T2B-tbl – sl1 to cable needle and hold in back, k-tbl, p1 from cable needle
- T2F-tbl – sl1 to cable needle and hold in front, p1, k-tbl from cable needle
- C2F – sl1 to cable needle and hold in front, k1, k1 from cable needle
- C3B – sl2 to cable needle and hold in back, k1, k2 from cable needle
- C3F – sl1 to cable needle and hold in front, k2, k1 from cable needle
- C4B – sl2 to cable needle and hold in back, k2, k2 from cable needle
- C4F – sl2 to cable needle and hold in front, k2, k2 from cable needle

Cuff

Round 1: Sl1, p1, k1, p2, k2, p2, k1, p1, sl1, [p1, k1] five times, p1, sl1, p1, k1, p2, k2, p2, k1, p1, sl1; [p1, k1, p1, sl1] seven times, p1, k1, p1.

Round 2: K1, p1, k1, p2, k2, p2, [k1, p1] eight times, k1, p2, k2, p2, k1, p1, k1; [p1, k1] 15 times, p1.

Repeat Rounds 1 & 2 for 1". Bind off all stitches using your favorite toe-up method. (I used the sewn bind-off.)

Vortex

Swirling cables take you into the knitterly vortex, not unlike what happens when you drop by one of those knitting-related-message-boards-which-shall-remain-unnamed (*cough*Ravelry!*cough*) for a quick peek and finally come up for air three hours later...

Materials:

Approximately 400 yards of fingering-weight yarn

Sample uses Nature's Palette Fingering Weight Merino (100% merino wool) in Dark Indigo.

US1 (2.25mm) needles or size needed to obtain gauge

Cable needle

Gauge:

9 stitches/12 rounds per inch in stockinette stitch

Size:

Foot circumference = approximately 8"

Toe

Using your favorite toe-up method, cast on six instep stitches and six heel stitches, dividing them over your selected needles. Place a marker at the start of the instep stitches to indicate the beginning of the round.

Round 1: K-fb, knit to last two instep stitches, k-fb, k1; repeat across heel stitches. 16 stitches.

Repeat Round 1 an additional four times. 32 stitches.

Next Round: K-fb, knit to last two instep stitches, k-fb, k1; repeat across heel stitches. 36 stitches.

Next Round: Knit.

Repeat last two rounds an additional nine times. 72 stitches.

Foot

Begin working the instep stitches in the *Spiral Cable Pattern* from chart on p. 102 or written instructions below while continuing to work the heel stitches in stockinette stitch. Work until the foot from the tip of the toe to the needles measures approximately 4^1/$_2$” less than the desired total length, ending with Round 2, 6, 10 or 14.

Spiral Cable Pattern:
(over 36 stitches and 16 rounds)

Rounds 1 & 2: P1, k2, sl1, [p2, k2] twice, p3, k2, p2, k2, p3, [k2, p2] twice, sl1, k2, p1.

Round 3: P1, C3B, p2, k2, [p2, T3F] twice, [T3B, p2] twice, k2, p2, C3F, p1.

Round 4: P1, k3, p2, [k2, p3] twice, k4, [p3, k2] twice, p2, k3, p1.

Round 5: P1, sl1, k2, p2, k2, p3, T3F, p2, C4F, p2, T3B, p3, k2, p2, k2, sl1, p1.

Round 6: P1, sl1, k2, p2, k2, p4, k2, p2, k4, p2, k2, p4, k2, p2, k2, sl1, p1.

Round 7: P1, C3F, p2, k2, p4, [T3F, T3B] twice, p4, k2, p2, C3B, p1.

Round 8: P1, k3, p2, k2, p5, k4, p2, k4, p5, k2, p2, k3, p1.

Round 9: P1, k2, sl1, p2, k2, p5, C4F, p2, C4F, p5, k2, p2, sl1, k2, p1.

Round 10: P1, k2, sl1, p2, k2, p5, k4, p2, k4, p5, k2, p2, sl1, k2, p1.

Round 11: P1, C3B, p2, k2, p4, [T3B, T3F] twice, p4, k2, p2, C3F, p1.

Round 12: P1, k3, p2, k2, p4, k2, p2, k4, p2, k2, p4, k2, p2, k3, p1.

Round 13: P1, sl1, k2, p2, k2, p3, T3B, p2, C4F, p2, T3F, p3, k2, p2, k2, sl1, p1.

Round 14: P1, sl1, k2, p2, [k2, p3] twice, k4, [p3, k2] twice, p2, k2, sl1, p1.

Round 15: P1, C3F, p2, k2, [p2, T3B] twice, [T3F, p2] twice, k2, p2, C3B, p1.

Round 16: P1, k3, [p2, k2] twice, p3, k2, p2, k2, p3, [k2, p2] twice, k3, p1.

Heel
Gusset

Round 1: Work instep stitches in *Spiral Cable Pattern* as established; k-fb in first heel stitch, knit to last two heel stitches, k-fb, k1.

Round 2: Continue working instep stitches in pattern; knit across heel stitches.

Repeat Rounds 1 & 2 an additional 15 times. 68 heel stitches.

Spiral Cable Pattern Chart

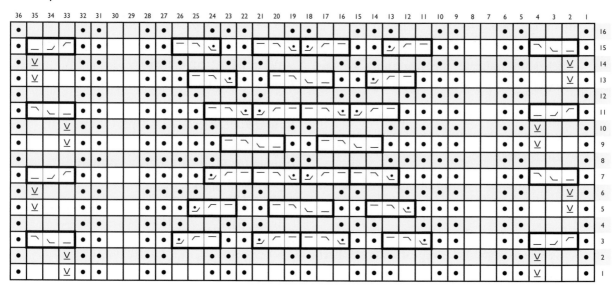

Slip Cable Pattern Chart

	knit
●	purl
Ⅴ	sl1
	T3B - sl1 to cable needle and hold in back, k2, p1 from cable needle
	T3F - sl2 to cable needle and hold in front, p1, k2 from cable needle
	C3B - sl2 to cable needle and hold in back, k1, k2 from cable needle
	C3F - sl1 to cable needle and hold in front, k2, k1 from cable needle
	C4F - sl2 to cable needle and hold in front, k2, k2 from cable needle

Turn Heel

Work across instep stitches in pattern. The heel turn will be worked back and forth on the 68 heel stitches.

Row 1 (RS): K51, W&T.

Row 2: P34, W&T.

Row 3: Knit to stitch before wrapped stitch (do not knit any wrapped stitches), W&T.

Row 4: Purl to stitch before wrapped stitch (do not purl any wrapped stitches), W&T.

Repeat Rows 3 & 4 an additional 10 times - there are now 12 wrapped stitches on either side of 12 unwrapped center stitches. Knit to end of heel stitches, lifting wraps RS as they are encountered, then work across instep stitches in pattern.

Heel Flap

Work the heel flap back and forth.

Row 1 (RS): K51, lifting remaining wraps RS, SSK, turn.

Row 2: [Sl1, p1] 17 times, sl1, p2tog, turn.

Row 3: Sl1, k34, SSK, turn.

Repeat Rows 2 & 3 an additional 14 times. Do not turn after working final repeat of Row 3 (one gusset stitch remains on right-hand edge of heel).

Next Round: Work across instep stitches in pattern; k2tog, knit to end of heel stitches. 36 heel stitches.

Leg

Continuing in the round, work the instep stitches in *Spiral Cable Pattern* as established. If the first instep round worked for the leg is Round 1 or Round 9, start the *Slip Cable Pattern* from chart on p. 102 or written instructions below on the back-of-leg/heel stitches with Round 1. If it's Round 5 or Round 13, start the *Slip Cable Pattern* with Round 5. Otherwise, work the back-of-leg/heel stitches in stockinette stitch until you reach one of these instep rounds so that the patterns will match up around the leg. End with Round 16 of *Spiral Cable Pattern* when leg is approximately 5" from the top of the heel flap or 1" less than desired finished length.

Slip Cable Pattern

(over 36 stitches and 8 rounds)

Rounds 1 & 2: P1, [k2, p2, sl1, k2, p2] twice, k2, sl1, [p2, k2] twice, sl1, p2, k2, p1.

Round 3: P1, [k2, p2, C3F, p2] twice, C3B, p2, k2, p2, C3B, p2, k2, p1.

Round 4: P1, [k2, p2, k3, p2] twice, k3, p2, k2, p2, k3, p2, k2, p1.

Rounds 5 & 6: P1, [k2, p1, k2, sl1, p2] twice, sl1, [k2, p2] twice, sl1, k2, p2, k2, p1.

Round 7: P1, [k2, p2, C3B, p2] twice, C3F, p2, k2, p2, C3F, p2, k2, p1.

Round 8: Repeat Round 4.

Cuff

Rounds 1 - 10: P1, k3, [p2, k2] twice, p3, k2, p2, k2, p3, [k2, p2] twice, k3, p1; p1, [k2, p2, k3, p2] twice, k3, p2, k2, p2, k3, p2, k2, p1.

Bind off all stitches using your favorite toe-up method. (I used the yarn over bind-off.)

Great Plains

This pattern was inspired by Buffalo Gold's incredible buffalo-down sock yarn, which knit into a sock that I find extremely hard to take off - it is incredibly soft and decadent. Due to its fuzziness and natural dark brown color, this yarn can be a bit challenging to design with. I chose a stitch pattern utilizing twisted stitches, smocking and eyelets that interplays nicely with the rustic character of the yarn. Choose a lighter-colored sport-weight yarn to make the textures really pop.

Materials:

Approximately 300 yards of sport-weight yarn

Sample uses Buffalo Gold #3 Sportweight Yarn (90% bison down, 10% nylon), undyed.

US2 (2.75mm) needles or size needed to obtain gauge

Cable needle or locking stitch marker

Gauge:

7 $^1/_2$ stitches/10 rounds per inch in stockinette stitch

Size:

Foot circumference = approximately 8"

Toe

Using your favorite toe-up method, cast on 29 instep stitches and 29 heel stitches, dividing them over your selected needles. The toe will be worked back and forth across the instep stitches.

Shape Bottom of Toe

Row 1 (RS): K28, W&T.

Row 2 (WS): P27, W&T.

Row 3: Knit to stitch before wrapped stitch (do not knit across any wrapped stitches), W&T.

Row 4: Purl to stitch before wrapped stitch (do not purl across any wrapped stitches), W&T.

Repeat Rows 3 & 4 an additional eight times - there are now 10 wrapped stitches on either side of 9 unwrapped center stitches.

Shape Top of Toe

Row 1 (RS): Knit to first wrapped stitch (do not knit across any wrapped stitches), lift wrap RS, turn.

Row 2 (WS): Sl1, purl to first wrapped stitch (do not purl across any wrapped stitches), lift wrap WS, turn.

Row 3: Sl1, knit to next wrapped stitch (just past the stitch unwrapped on the previous RS row), lift wrap RS, turn.

Row 4: Sl1, purl to next wrapped stitch (just past the stitch unwrapped on the previous WS row), lift wrap WS, turn.

Repeat Rows 3 & 4 an additional seven times - a single wrapped stitch remains on either side of toe.

Next Round: Sl1, k27, lift wrap RS, but do not turn; knit across heel stitches.

Next Round: Lift wrap RS to hide the final wrap (which is at the beginning of the round), m1, knit to last instep stitch, m1, k1; knit to end of heel stitches. 60 stitches, 31 instep and 29 heel.

Foot

Begin to work the instep stitches in *Great Plains Lace* from chart on p. 108 or written instructions below while continuing to work the heel stitches in stockinette stitch. Work until the foot from the tip of the toe to the needles measures approximately 2" less than the desired total length, ending with Round 12 or 26 of pattern.

 Cluster Stitch: With yarn in front, slip next five stitches to cable needle. Wrap yarn around the base of these five stitches three times by bringing yarn to front between right needle and cable needle, bringing yarn to back between left needle and cable needle, and repeating two more times. After stitches are wrapped and yarn is brought to the back for the last time, k-tbl, p1, k-tbl, p1, k-tbl from cable needle.

Great Plains Lace:
(over 31 stitches and 28 rounds)

Round 1: [P2, k-tbl] three times, p2, [SSK, YO] four times, k1, [p2, k-tbl] three times, p2.

Round 2: [P2, k-tbl] three times, p2, k9, [p2, k-tbl] three times, p2.

Round 3: [P2, k-tbl] three times, p2, k1, [YO, k2tog] four times, [p2, k-tbl] three times, p2.

Round 4: Repeat Round 2.

Round 5: P2, T2F-tbl, p1, k-tbl, p1, T2B-tbl, p2, [SSK, YO] four times, k1, p2, T2F-tbl, p1, k-tbl, p1, T2B-tbl, p2.

Round 6: P3, [k-tbl, p1] twice, k-tbl, p3, k9, p3, [k-tbl, p1] twice, k-tbl, p3.

Round 7: P3, cluster stitch, p3, k1, [YO, k2tog] four times, p3, cluster stitch, p3.

Round 8: Repeat Round 6.

Round 9: P2, T2B-tbl, p1, k-tbl, p1, T2F-tbl, p2, [SSK, YO] four times, k1, p2, T2B-tbl, p1, k-tbl, p1, T2F-tbl, p2.

Rounds 10 - 12: Repeat Rounds 2 - 4.

Round 13: P1, T2B-tbl, p2, k-tbl, p2, T2F-tbl, p1, T2F-tbl, p2, k-tbl, p2, T2B-tbl, p1, T2B-tbl, p2, k-tbl, p2, T2F-tbl, p1.

Round 14: P1, k9, [p2, k-tbl] three times, p2, k9, p1.

Round 15: P1, [SSK, YO] four times, k1, [p2, k-tbl] three times, p2, [SSK, YO] four times, k1, p1.

Round 16: Repeat Round 14.

Round 17: P1, k1, [YO, k2tog] four times, [p2, k-tbl] three times, p2, k1, [YO, k2tog] four times, p1.

Round 18: Repeat Round 14.

Round 19: P1, [SSK, YO] four times, k1, p2, T2F-tbl, p1, k-tbl, p1, T2B-tbl, p2, [SSK, YO] four times, k1, p1.

Round 20: P1, k9, p3, [k-tbl, p1] twice, k-tbl, p3, k9, p1.

Round 21: P1, k1, [YO, k2tog] four times, p3, cluster stitch, p3, k1, [YO, k2tog] four times, p1.

Round 22: Repeat Round 20.

Round 23: P1, [SSK, YO] four times, k1, p2, T2B-tbl, p1, k-tbl, p1, T2F-tbl, p2, [SSK, YO] four times, k1, p1.

Rounds 24 - 26: Repeat Rounds 16 - 18.

Round 27: P1, T2F-tbl, p2, k-tbl, p2, T2B-tbl, p1, T2B-tbl, p2, k-tbl, p2, T2F-tbl, p1, T2F-tbl, p2, k-tbl, p2, T2B-tbl, p1.

Round 28: Repeat Round 2.

Heel

Work across instep stitches in pattern. The heel will be worked back and forth over the 29 heel stitches.

Shape Bottom of Heel

Row 1 (RS): K28, W&T.

Row 2 (WS): P27, W&T.

Row 3: Knit to stitch before wrapped stitch (do not knit across any wrapped stitches), W&T.

Row 4: Purl to stitch before wrapped stitch (do not purl across any wrapped stitches), W&T.

Repeat Rows 3 & 4 an additional eight times - there are now 10 wrapped stitches on either side of 9 unwrapped center stitches.

Shape Top of Heel

Row 1 (RS): Knit to first wrapped stitch (do not knit across any wrapped stitches), lift wrap RS, turn.

Row 2 (WS): Sl1, purl to first wrapped stitch (do not purl across any wrapped stitches), lift wrap WS, turn.

Row 3: Sl1, knit to next wrapped stitch (just past the stitch unwrapped on the previous RS row), lift wrap RS, turn.

Row 4: Sl1, purl to next wrapped stitch (just past the stitch unwrapped on the previous WS row), lift wrap WS, turn.

Repeat Rows 3 & 4 an additional seven times - a single wrapped stitch remains on either side of heel.

Next Row: Sl1, knit to last wrapped stitch, lift wrap RS, but do not turn. You should be at the beginning of the instep stitches.

Next Round: Work instep stitches in pattern as established; lift wrap RS, knit to end of heel stitches.

Leg

Continuing in the round, work *Great Plains Lace* from chart on p. 108 (working the outlined pattern repeat around the entire leg) or written instructions below, making sure to work the next round in sequence based on where you ended before turning the heel. End with Round 12 or 26 of pattern when leg measures approximately 5" from top of heel or 1" less than desired finished length.

Great Plains Lace for Leg:
(over 60 stitches and 28 rounds)

Round 1: *[P2, k-tbl] three times, p2, [SSK, YO] four times, k1; repeat from * to end of round.

Round 2: *[P2, k-tbl] three times, p2, k9; repeat from * to end of round.

Round 3: *[P2, k-tbl] three times, p2, k1, [YO, k2tog] four times; repeat from * to end of round.

Round 4: Repeat Round 2.

Round 5: *P2, T2F-tbl, p1, k-tbl, p1, T2B-tbl, p2, [SSK, YO] four times, k1; repeat from * to end of round.

Round 6: *P3, [k-tbl, p1] twice, k-tbl, p3, k9; repeat from * to end of round.

Round 7: *P3, cluster stitch, p3, k1, [YO, k2tog] four times; repeat from * to end of round.

Round 8: Repeat Round 6.

Round 9: *P2, T2B-tbl, p1, k-tbl, p1, T2F-tbl, p2, [SSK, YO] four times, k1; repeat from * to end of round.

Rounds 10 - 12: Repeat Rounds 2 - 4.

Round 13: *P1, T2B-tbl, p2, k-tbl, p2, T2F-tbl, p1, T2F-tbl, p2, k-tbl, p2, T2B-tbl; repeat from * to end of round.

Round 14: *P1, k9, [p2, k-tbl] three times, p1; repeat from * to end of round.

Round 15: *P1, [SSK, YO] four times, k1, [p2, k-tbl] three times, p1; repeat from * to end of round.

Round 16: Repeat Round 14.

Round 17: *P1, k1, [YO, k2tog] four times, [p2, k-tbl] three times, p1; repeat from * to end of round.

Round 18: Repeat Round 14.

Round 19: *P1, [SSK, YO] four times, k1, p2, T2F-tbl, p1, k-tbl, p1, T2B-tbl, p1; repeat from * to end of round.

Round 20: *P1, k9, p3, [k-tbl, p1] twice, k-tbl, p2; repeat from * to end of round.

Round 21: *P1, k1, [YO, k2tog] four times, p3, cluster stitch, p2; repeat from * to end of round.

Round 22: Repeat Round 20.

Round 23: *P1, [SSK, YO] four times, k1, p2, T2B-tbl, p1, k-tbl, p1, T2F-tbl, p1; repeat from * to end of round.

Rounds 24 - 26: Repeat Rounds 16 - 18.

Round 27: *P1, T2F-tbl, p2, k-tbl, p2, T2B-tbl, p1, T2B-tbl, p2, k-tbl, p2, T2F-tbl; repeat from * to end of round.

Round 28: Repeat Round 2.

Cuff

Round 1: *[P2, k-tbl] three times, p3, [k-tbl, p2] twice, k-tbl, p1; repeat from * to end of round.

Repeat Round 1 an additional seven times. Bind off all stitches using your favorite toe-up method. (I used the p2tog bind-off.)

Great Plains Lace Chart

(chart grid, columns numbered 31–1 across the top, rows numbered 28–1 down the right side)

Legend:

- ☐ knit
- ⊡ purl
- B k-tbl
- O YO
- ⋀ SSK
- ⋀ k2tog
- T2B-tbl – sl1 to cable needle and hold in back, k-tbl, p1 from cable needle
- T2F-tbl – sl1 to cable needle and hold in front, p1, k-tbl from cable needle
- B•B•B cluster stitch
- ☐ pattern repeat

108   Toe-Up!

Spring in Oregon

These socks were modeled after the best-selling Autumn in Oregon Socks from my Gardiner Yarn Works pattern line, which is knit top-down. I decided that the falling leaves looked like sprouting shoots when turned upside down, and Spring in Oregon was born!

Materials:

Approximately 400 yards of fingering-weight yarn

Sample uses Shibui Sock (100% superwash merino wool) in Kiwi.

US1 (2.25mm) needles or size needed to obtain gauge, with an extra needle for attaching the cuff

Gauge:

9 stitches/11 rounds per inch in stockinette stitch

Size:

Foot circumference = approximately 8"

Toe

Using your favorite toe-up method, cast on seven instep stitches and seven heel stitches, dividing them over your selected needles. Place a marker at the start of the instep stitches to indicate the beginning of the round.

Work Rounds 1 - 23 from *Toe Chart - Instep* on p. 112 or written instructions for toe below. If working from chart, the uncharted heel/bottom-of-foot stitches will be worked in stockinette, with increases in the first and second-to-last stitches of the even-numbered rounds to match the instep increases. If you prefer not to have texture on the top of your toe, work toe stitches in stockinette as well, placing increases as for bottom of foot.

Round 1: Knit.

Round 2: K-fb, k4, k-fb, k1; repeat across heel stitches. 18 stitches, 9 instep and 9 heel.

Round 3: Knit.

Round 4: K-fb, k6, k-fb, k1; repeat across heel stitches. 22 stitches, 11 instep and 11 heel.

Round 5: K2, [k-tbl, p2] twice, k-tbl, k2; knit across heel stitches.

Round 6: K-fb, k1, k-tbl, p2, inc4 (see chart key on p. 112), p2, k-tbl, k-fb, k1; k-fb, k8, k-fb, k1. 30 stitches, 17 instep and 13 heel.

Round 7: K3, k-tbl, p2, k5, p2, k-tbl, k3; knit across heel stitches.

Round 8: K-fb, k2, k-tbl, p2, k5, p2, k-tbl, k1, k-fb, k1; k-fb, k10, k-fb, k1. 34 stitches, 19 instep and 15 heel.

Round 9: K4, k-tbl, p2, SSK, k1, k2tog, p2, k-tbl, k4; knit across heel stitches. 32 stitches, 17 instep and 15 heel.

Round 10: K-fb, k3, k-tbl, p2, k3, p2, k-tbl, k2, k-fb, k1; k-fb, k12, k-fb, k1. 36 stitches, 19 instep and 17 heel.

Round 11: K2, [k-tbl, p2] twice, S2KP, [p2, k-tbl] twice, k2; knit across heel stitches. 34 stitches, 17 instep and 17 heel.

Round 12: K-fb, k1, k-tbl, p2, inc4, p2, k-tbl, p2, inc4, p2, k-tbl, k-fb, k1; k-fb, k14, k-fb, k1. 46 stitches, 27 instep and 19 heel.

Round 13: K3, [k-tbl, p2, k5, p2] twice, k-tbl, k3; knit across heel stitches.

Round 14: K-fb, k2, [k-tbl, p2, k5, p2] twice, k-tbl, k1, k-fb, k1; k-fb, k16, k-fb, k1. 50 stitches, 29 instep and 21 heel.

Round 15: K2, [p2, k-tbl, p2, SSK, k1, k2tog] twice, p2, k-tbl, p2, k2; knit across heel stitches. 46 stitches, 25 instep and 21 heel.

Round 16: K-fb, k1, [p2, k-tbl, p2, k3] twice, p2, k-tbl, p2, k-fb, k1; k-fb, k18, k-fb, k1. 50 stitches, 27 instep and 23 heel.

Round 17: K3, [p2, k-tbl, p2, S2KP] twice, p2, k-tbl, p2, k3; knit across heel stitches. 46 stitches, 23 instep and 23 heel.

Round 18: K-fb, k2, p2, inc4, [p2, k-tbl] three times, p2, inc4, p2, k1, k-fb, k1; k-fb, k20, k-fb, k1. 58 stitches, 33 instep and 25 heel.

Round 19: K4, p2, k5, [p2, k-tbl] three times, p2, k5, p2, k4; knit across heel stitches.

Round 20: K-fb, k3, p2, k5, [p2, k-tbl] three times, p2, k5, p2, k2, k-fb, k1; k-fb, k22, k-fb, k1. 62 stitches, 35 instep and 27 heel.

Round 21: K5, p2, SSK, k1, k2tog, [p2, k-tbl] three times, p2, SSK, k1, k2tog, p2, k5; knit across heel stitches. 58 stitches, 31 instep and 27 heel.

Round 22: K-fb, k4, p2, k3, [p2, k-tbl] three times, p2, k3, p2, k3, k-fb, k1; k-fb, k24, k-fb, k1. 62 stitches, 33 instep and 29 heel.

Round 23: K6, p2, S2KP, [p2, k-tbl] three times, p2, S2KP, p2, k6; knit across heel stitches. 58 stitches, 29 instep and 29 heel.

Foot

Begin working the instep stitches in the *Sprout Pattern* from chart on p. 113 or written instructions below while continuing to work the heel stitches in stockinette stitch. Work until the foot from the tip of the toe to the needles measures approximately 2" less than the desired total length.

Sprout Pattern:
(over 29 stitches and 18 rounds)

Round 1: K2, [p1, k1] twice, p2, [k-tbl, p2] twice, inc4, [p2, k-tbl] twice, p2, [k1, p1] twice, k2.

Round 2: [K1, p1] twice, k2, p2, [k-tbl, p2] twice, k5, [p2, k-tbl] twice, p2, k2, [p1, k1] twice.

Round 3: K2, [p1, k1] twice, p2, [k-tbl, p2] twice, k5, [p2, k-tbl] twice, p2, [k1, p1] twice, k2.

Round 4: [K1, p1] twice, k2, p2, [k-tbl, p2] twice, SSK, k1, k2tog, [p2, k-tbl] twice, p2, k2, [p1, k1] twice.

Round 5: K2, [p1, k1] twice, p2, [k-tbl, p2] twice, k3, [p2, k-tbl] twice, p2, [k1, p1] twice, k2.

Round 6: [K1, p1] twice, k2, p2, [k-tbl, p2] twice, S2KP, [p2, k-tbl] twice, p2, k2, [p1, k1] twice.

Round 7: K2, [p1, k1] twice, [p2, k-tbl, p2, inc4] twice, p2, k-tbl, p2, [k1, p1] twice, k2.

Round 8: [K1, p1] twice, k2, [p2, k-tbl, p2, k5] twice, p2, k-tbl, p2, k2, [p1, k1] twice.

Round 9: K2, [p1, k1] twice, [p2, k-tbl, p2, k5] twice, p2, k-tbl, p2, [k1, p1] twice, k2.

Round 10: [K1, p1] twice, k2, [p2, k-tbl, p2, SSK, k1, k2tog] twice, p2, k-tbl, p2, k2, [p1, k1] twice.

Round 11: K2, [p1, k1] twice, [p2, k-tbl, p2, k3] twice, p2, k-tbl, p2, [k1, p1] twice, k2.

Round 12: [K1, p1] twice, k2, [p2, k-tbl, p2, S2KP] twice, p2, k-tbl, p2, k2, [p1, k1] twice.

Round 13: K2, [p1, k1] twice, p2, inc4, [p2, k-tbl] three times, p2, inc4, p2, [k1, p1] twice, k2.

Round 14: [K1, p1] twice, k2, p2, k5, [p2, k-tbl] three times, p2, k5, p2, k2, [p1, k1] twice.

Round 15: K2, [p1, k1] twice, p2, k5, [p2, k-tbl] three times, p2, k5, p2, [k1, p1] twice, k2.

Round 16: [K1, p1] twice, k2, p2, SSK, k1, k2tog, [p2, k-tbl] three times, p2, SSK, k1, k2tog, p2, k2, [p1, k1] twice.

Round 17: K2, [p1, k1] twice, p2, k3, [p2, k-tbl] three times, p2, k3, p2, [k1, p1] twice, k2.

Round 18: [K1, p1] twice, k2, p2, S2KP, [p2, k-tbl] three times, p2, S2KP, p2, k2, [p1, k1] twice.

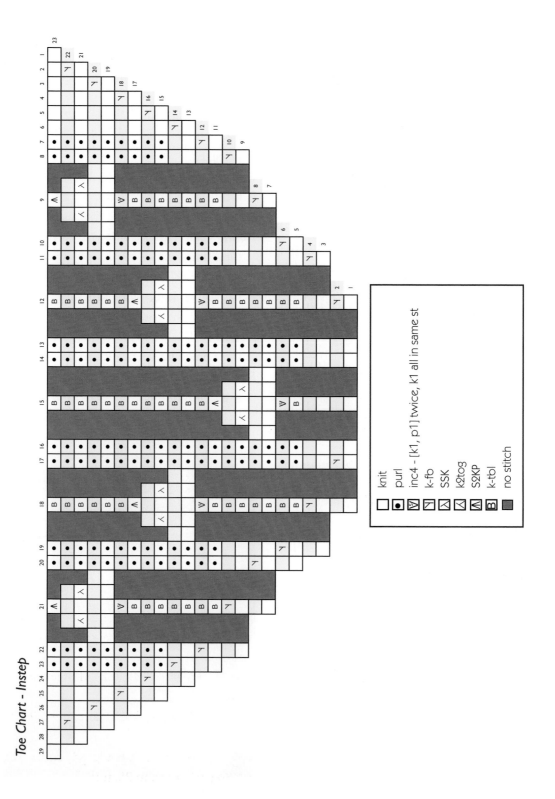

Toe Chart - Instep

		knit
		purl
		inc4 - [k1, p1] twice, k1 all in same st
		k-fb
		SSK
		k2tog
		S2KP
		k-tbl
		no stitch

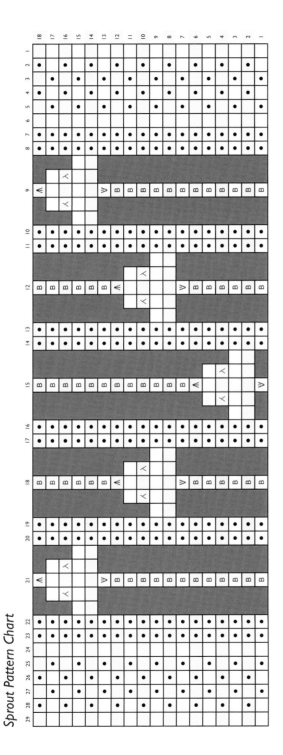

Sprout Pattern Chart

Heel

Work across instep stitches in pattern. The heel will be worked back and forth on the 29 heel stitches.

Shape Bottom of Heel

Row 1 (RS): Knit to last stitch on needle, W&T.

Row 2: Purl to last stitch on needle, W&T.

Row 3: Knit to stitch before wrapped stitch (do not knit across any wrapped stitches), W&T.

Row 4: Purl to stitch before wrapped stitch (do not purl across any wrapped stitches), W&T.

Repeat Rows 3 & 4 an additional eight times - there are now ten wrapped stitches on either side of nine unwrapped center stitches.

Shape Top of Heel

Work Rows 1 - 19 and Round 20 from *Heel Flap Pattern* chart on p. 115 or written instructions.

Heel Flap Pattern

Row 1 (RS): P4, YO, p2tog, p3, lift wrap RS, turn.

Row 2: Sl1, k4, p1, k4, lift wrap WS, turn.

Row 3: Sl1, p4, k1, p5, lift wrap RS, turn.

Row 4: Sl1, k5, p1, k5, lift wrap WS, turn.

Row 5: Sl1, p5, k1, p6, lift wrap RS, turn.

Row 6: Sl1, k6, p1, k6, lift wrap WS, turn.

Row 7: Sl1, p3, YO, p2tog, p4, YO, p2tog, p3, lift wrap RS, turn.

Row 8: Sl1, k4, p1, k5, p1, k4, lift wrap WS, turn.

Row 9: Sl1, p4, [k1, p5] twice, lift wrap RS, turn.

Row 10: Sl1, [k5, p1] twice, k5, lift wrap WS, turn.

Row 11: Sl1, [p5, k1] twice, p6, lift wrap RS, turn.

Row 12: Sl1, k6, p1, k5, p1, k6, lift wrap WS, turn.

Row 13: Sl1, p3, [YO, p2tog, p4] twice, YO, p2tog, p3, lift wrap RS, turn.

Row 14: Sl1, k4, p1, [k5, p1] twice, k4, lift wrap WS, turn.

Row 15: Sl1, p4, [k1, p5] three times, lift wrap RS, turn.

Row 16: Sl1, [k5, p1] three times, k5, lift wrap WS, turn.

Row 17: Sl1, [p5, k1] three times, p6, lift wrap RS, turn.

Row 18: Sl1, k6, [p1, k5] twice, p1, k6, lift wrap WS, turn.

Row 19: Sl1, p3, [YO, p2tog, p4] three times, YO, p2tog, p3, lift wrap RS, but do not turn.

Round 20: Work across instep stitches in pattern; lift wrap RS, p4, [k1, p5] four times.

Leg

Continuing in the round, work the instep stitches continuing in *Sprout Pattern* and the back-of-leg stitches in *Raindrop Pattern* from the chart on p. 115 or written instructions below. End with Round 6 of the *Sprout Pattern* when leg is approximately 7" from the bottom (Row 1) of the heel.

Raindrop Pattern:
(over 29 stitches and 12 rounds)

Rounds 1 - 4: [P5, k1] four times, p5.

Round 5: P2, [YO, p2tog, p4] four times, YO, p2tog, p1.

Rounds 6 - 10: P2, [k1, p5] four times, k1, p2.

Round 11: P5, [YO, p2tog, p4] four times.

Round 12: [P5, k1] four times, p5.

Cuff

Round 1: K7, m1, [k11, m1] four times, k7, m1. 64 stitches. Break yarn.

At this point, you are done working your leg in the round. If you are working on two circular needles, you can transfer all of your leg stitches onto a single needle. If you are

using one long circular, you can pull out your loops and let all of the stitches rest on the cable. To knit the cuff onto the sock leg, you will need an extra needle, either the unused end of your circular or an empty dpn.

Arrange your stitches so that the start of the new round is in the center back of the leg. The cuff seam should be centered at the top of the *Raindrop Pattern,* with the right-hand needle holding active stitches to knit the cuff onto, starting with heel stitch #15. Using a provisional cast-on (see glossary), place eight new stitches on an empty needle (these stitches will not be attached to the leg of the sock until the SSK join at the end of Row 1 of the cuff pattern).

Begin working the *Leaf Lace Cuff Pattern* back and forth across these eight stitches from the chart or written instructions on p. 116. You will work Rows 2 - 19 a total of seven times to complete the circle.

Toe-Up!

Raindrop Pattern Chart

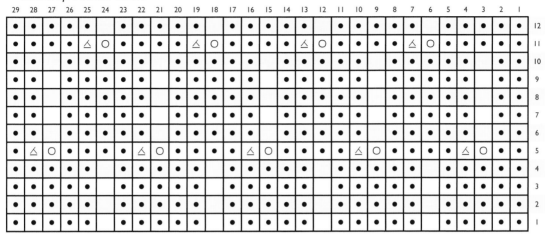

Heel Flap Pattern Chart

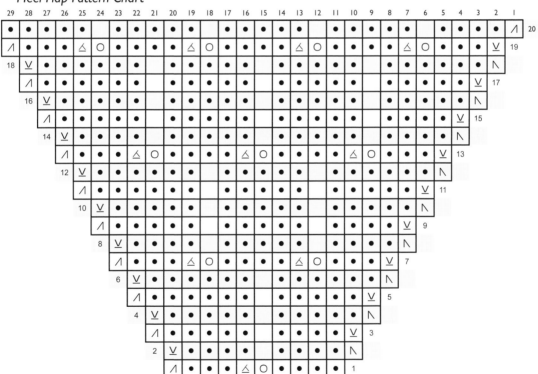

	knit on RS, purl on WS		sl1
	purl on RS, knit on WS		lift wrap RS
	YO		lift wrap WS
	p2tog		

Leaf Lace Cuff Pattern:

Row 1 (WS): K2, p1, k4, SSK join (SSK using one stitch from the cuff and one from the leg of the sock with WS facing).

Row 2: Sl1, k4, YO, k1, YO, k2. 10 cuff stitches.

Row 3: P6, k-fb, k2, SSK join. 11 cuff stitches.

Row 4: Sl1, k3, p1, k2, YO, k1, YO, k3. 13 cuff stitches.

Row 5: P8, k-fb, k3, SSK join. 14 cuff stitches.

Row 6: Sl1, k3, p2, k3, YO, k1, YO, k4. 16 cuff stitches.

Row 7: P10, k-fb, k4, SSK join. 17 cuff stitches.

Row 8: Sl1, k3, p3, k4, YO, k1, YO, k5. 19 cuff stitches.

Row 9: P12, k-fb, k5, SSK join. 20 cuff stitches.

Row 10: Sl1, k3, p4, SSK, k7, k2tog, k1. 18 cuff stitches.

Row 11: P10, k-fb, k6, SSK join. 19 cuff stitches.

Row 12: Sl1, k3, p5, SSK, k5, k2tog, k1. 17 cuff stitches.

Row 13: P8, k-fb, k7, SSK join. 18 cuff stitches.

Row 14: Sl1, k3, p1, k1, p4, SSK, k3, k2tog, k1. 16 cuff stitches.

Row 15: P6, k-fb, k3, p1, k4, SSK join. 17 cuff stitches.

Row 16: Sl1, k3, p1, k1, p5, SSK, k1, k2tog, k1. 15 cuff stitches.

Row 17: P4, k-fb, k4, p1, k4, SSK join. 16 cuff stitches.

Row 18: Sl1, k3, p1, k1, p6, SK2P, k1. 14 cuff stitches.

Row 19: P2tog, bind off next five stitches, k1, p1, k4, SSK join. 8 cuff stitches.

Repeat Rows 2 - 19 until all leg stitches are used up. Carefully remove the provisional cast-on, place the live stitches on an empty needle, and graft the cuff closed using Kitchener Stitch.

Leaf Lace Cuff Pattern Chart

	knit on RS, purl on WS
●	purl on RS, knit on WS
V	sl1 with yarn in back
	k-fb
	SSK (when doing this at join between cuff and leg, take one stitch from each)
	k2tog
O	YO
	SK2P
	p2tog
X	bind off by knitting next stitch and passing right-hand stitch over it
	pattern repeat

Peace Lily

I found this stitch pattern and designed this sock to express my hope for a peaceful planet. In these challenging days of war and unrest, it's difficult to see how we will reach that goal, but I can't help wanting it for my kids. This sock is dedicated to the next generation in hopes that the human race can resolve its differences with a minimum of heartache.

Materials:

Approximately 400 yards of fingering-weight yarn

Sample uses Lavender Sheep Silky Sock (50% merino wool, 50% silk) in Peace Lily.

US1 (2.25mm) needles or size needed to obtain gauge

Cable needle

Gauge:

8 stitches/10 rounds per inch in stockinette stitch

Size:

Foot circumference = approximately 7 1/2"

Toe

Using your favorite toe-up method, cast on 32 instep stitches and 32 heel stitches, dividing them over your selected needles. The toe will be worked back and forth across the instep stitches.

Shape Bottom of Toe

Row 1 (RS): K31, W&T.

Row 2 (WS): P30, W&T.

Row 3: Knit to stitch before wrapped stitch (do not knit across any wrapped stitches), W&T.

Row 4: Purl to stitch before wrapped stitch (do not purl across any wrapped stitches), W&T.

Repeat Rows 3 & 4 an additional nine times - there are now 11 wrapped stitches on either side of ten unwrapped center stitches.

Shape Top of Toe

Row 1 (RS): Knit to first wrapped stitch (do not knit across any wrapped stitches), lift wrap RS, turn.

Row 2 (WS): Sl1, purl to first wrapped stitch (do not purl across any wrapped stitches), lift wrap WS, turn.

Row 3: Sl1, knit to next wrapped stitch (just past the stitch unwrapped on the previous RS row), lift wrap RS, turn.

Row 4: Sl1, purl to next wrapped stitch (just past the stitch unwrapped on the previous WS row), lift wrap WS, turn.

Repeat Rows 3 & 4 an additional eight times - a single wrapped stitch remains on either side of toe.

Next Round: Sl1, k30, lift wrap RS, but do not turn; knit across heel stitches.

Next Round: Lift wrap RS to hide the final wrap (which is at the beginning of the round), then knit the rest of the round even.

Foot

Begin to work the instep stitches in *Peace Lily Pattern for Instep* from chart on p. 120 or written instructions below while continuing to work the heel stitches in stockinette stitch. Work until the foot from the tip of the toe to the needles measures approximately 2" less than the desired total length.

Peace Lily Pattern for Instep:

(over 32 stitches and 32 rounds)

Rounds 1 & 2: K4, p3, k-tbl twice, p3, k8, p3, k-tbl twice, p3, k4.

Round 3: K3, p3, T2B-tbl, T2F-tbl, p3, k6, p3, T2B-tbl, T2F-tbl, p3, k3.

Round 4: K3, p3, k-tbl, p2, k-tbl, p3, k6, p3, k-tbl, p2, k-tbl, p3, k3.

Round 5: K2, p3, T2B-tbl, p2, T2F-tbl, p3, k4, p3, T2B-tbl, p2, T2F-tbl, p3, k2.

Round 6: K2, p3, k-tbl, p4, k-tbl, p3, k4, p3, k-tbl, p4, k-tbl, p3, k2.

Round 7: K1, p3, T2B-tbl, p4, T2F-tbl, p3, k2, p3, T2B-tbl, p4, T2F-tbl, p3, k1.

Round 8: K1, p3, k-tbl, p6, k-tbl, p3, k2, p3, k-tbl, p6, k-tbl, p3, k1.

Round 9: P3, T2B-tbl, p6, T2F-tbl, p6, T2B-tbl, p6, T2F-tbl, p3.

Round 10: P3, k-tbl, p8, k-tbl, p6, k-tbl, p8, k-tbl, p3.

Round 11: P2, T2B-tbl, p8, T2F-tbl, p4, T2B-tbl, p8, T2F-tbl, p2.

Round 12: P2, k-tbl, p3, k4, p3, k-tbl, p4, k-tbl, p3, k4, p3, k-tbl, p2.

Round 13: P1, T2B-tbl, p3, C4F, p3, T2F-tbl, p2, T2B-tbl, p3, C4F, p3, T2F-tbl, p1.

Round 14: P1, k-tbl, p4, k4, p4, k-tbl, p2, k-tbl, p4, k4, p4, k-tbl, p1.

Round 15: *T2B-tbl, p2, C4B, C4F, p2, T2F-tbl; repeat from *.

Rounds 16 - 18: *K-tbl, p3, k8, p3, k-tbl; repeat from *.

Round 19: *T2F-tbl, p3, k6, p3, T2B-tbl; repeat from *.

Round 20: P1, k-tbl, p3, k6, p3, k-tbl, p2, k-tbl, p3, k6, p3, k-tbl, p1.

Round 21: P1, T2F-tbl, p3, k4, p3, T2B-tbl, p2, T2F-tbl, p3, k4, p3, T2B-tbl, p1.

Round 22: P2, k-tbl, p3, k4, p3, k-tbl, p4, k-tbl, p3, k4, p3, k-tbl, p2.

Round 23: P2, T2F-tbl, p3, k2, p3, T2B-tbl, p4, T2F-tbl, p3, k2, p3, T2B-tbl, p2.

Round 24: P3, k-tbl, p3, k2, p3, k-tbl, p6, k-tbl, p3, k2, p3, k-tbl, p3.

Round 25: P3, T2F-tbl, p6, T2B-tbl, p6, T2F-tbl, p6, T2B-tbl, p3.

Round 26: P4, k-tbl, p6, k-tbl, p8, k-tbl, p6, k-tbl, p4.

Round 27: P4, T2F-tbl, p4, T2B-tbl, p8, T2F-tbl, p4, T2B-tbl, p4.

Round 28: K2, p3, k-tbl, p4, k-tbl, p3, k4, p3, k-tbl, p4, k-tbl, p3, k2.

Round 29: K2, p3, T2F-tbl, p2, T2B-tbl, p3, C4F, p3, T2F-tbl, p2, T2B-tbl, p3, k2.

Round 30: *K2, p4, k-tbl, p2, k-tbl, p4, k2; repeat from *.

Round 31: *C4F, p2, T2F-tbl, T2B-tbl, p2, C4B; repeat from *.

Round 32: K4, p3, k-tbl twice, p3, k8, p3, k-tbl twice, p3, k4.

Heel

Work next round of *Peace Lily Pattern for Instep* across instep stitches. The heel will be worked back and forth over the 32 heel stitches.

Shape Bottom of Heel

Row 1 (RS): K31, W&T.

Row 2 (WS): P30, W&T.

Row 3: Knit to stitch before wrapped stitch (do not knit across any wrapped stitches), W&T.

Row 4: Purl to stitch before wrapped stitch (do not purl across any wrapped stitches), W&T.

Repeat Rows 3 & 4 an additional nine times - there are now 11 wrapped stitches on either side of ten unwrapped center stitches.

Shape Top of Heel

Row 1 (RS): Knit to first wrapped stitch (do not knit across any wrapped stitches), lift wrap RS, turn.

Row 2 (WS): Sl1, purl to first wrapped stitch (do not purl across any wrapped stitches), lift wrap WS, turn.

Row 3: Sl1, knit to next wrapped stitch (just past the stitch unwrapped on the previous RS row), lift wrap RS, turn.

Row 4: Sl1, purl to next wrapped stitch (just past the stitch unwrapped on the previous WS row), lift wrap WS, turn.

Repeat Rows 3 & 4 an additional eight times - a single wrapped stitch remains on either side of heel.

Next Row: Sl1, k30, lift wrap RS, but do not turn. You should be at the beginning of the instep stitches.

Next Round: Work next round of *Peace Lily Pattern for Instep* across instep stitches; lift wrap RS, knit to end of heel stitches.

Leg

Continuing in the round, work the *Peace Lily Pattern for Leg* from chart on p. 121 or written instructions on p. 122, making sure to work the next round in sequence based on where you ended before turning the heel. End with Round 1 or 17 of pattern when leg measures approximately 5" from top of heel.

Peace Lily Pattern for Instep Chart

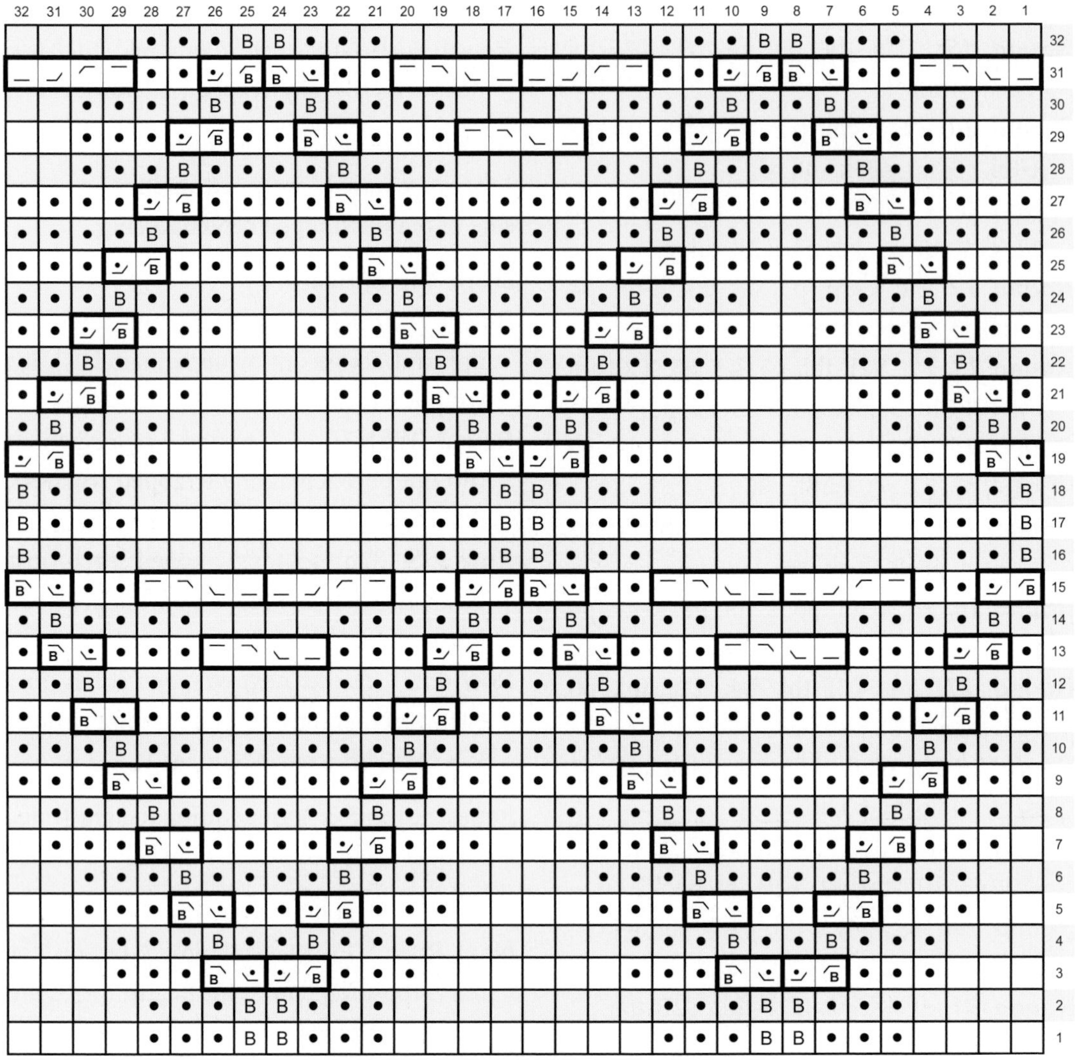

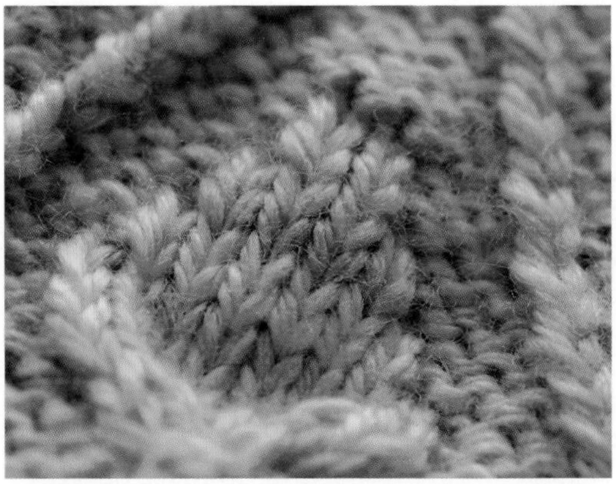

Peace Lily Pattern for Leg Chart

64 63 62 61 60 59 58 57 56 55 54 53 52 51 50 49 16 15 14 13 12 11 10 9 8 7 6 5 4 3 2 1

Legend:

- ☐ knit
- ● purl
- B k-tbl
- T2B-tbl - sl1 to cable needle and hold in back, k-tbl, p1 from cable needle
- T2F-tbl - sl1 to cable needle and hold in front, p1, k-tbl from cable needle
- C4F - sl2 to cable needle and hold in front, k2, k2 from cable needle
- C4B - sl2 to cable needle and hold in back, k2, k2 from cable needle
- pattern repeat

Note: At the end of Round 28, the C4F will be worked half on the last two sts of Round 28 and half on the first two sts of Round 29.

Peace Lily Pattern for Leg:
(over 64 stitches and 32 rounds)

Rounds 1 & 2: K4, [p3, k-tbl twice, p3, k8] three times, p3, k-tbl twice, p3, k4.

Round 3: K3, [p3, T2B-tbl, T2F-tbl, p3, k6] three times, p3, T2B-tbl, T2F-tbl, p3, k3.

Round 4: K3, [p3, k-tbl, p2, k-tbl, p3, k6] three times, p3, k-tbl, p2, k-tbl, p3, k3.

Round 5: K2, [p3, T2B-tbl, p2, T2F-tbl, p3, k4] three times, p3, T2B-tbl, p2, T2F-tbl, p3, k2.

Round 6: K2, [p3, k-tbl, p4, k-tbl, p3, k4] three times, p3, k-tbl, p4, k-tbl, p3, k2.

Round 7: K1, [p3, T2B-tbl, p4, T2F-tbl, p3, k2] three times, p3, T2B-tbl, p4, T2F-tbl, p3, k1.

Round 8: K1, [p3, k-tbl, p6, k-tbl, p3, k2] three times, p3, k-tbl, p6, k-tbl, p3, k1.

Round 9: P3, [T2B-tbl, p6, T2F-tbl, p6] three times, T2B-tbl, p6, T2F-tbl, p3.

Round 10: P3, [k-tbl, p8, k-tbl, p6] three times, k-tbl, p8, k-tbl, p3.

Round 11: P2, [T2B-tbl, p8, T2F-tbl, p4] three times, T2B-tbl, p8, T2F-tbl, p2.

Round 12: P2, [k-tbl, p3, k4, p3, k-tbl, p4] three times, k-tbl, p3, k4, p3, k-tbl, p2.

Round 13: P1, [T2B-tbl, p3, C4F, p3, T2F-tbl, p2] three times, T2B-tbl, p3, C4F, p3, T2F-tbl, p1.

Round 14: P1, [k-tbl, p4, k4, p4, k-tbl, p2] three times, k-tbl, p4, k4, p4, k-tbl, p1.

Round 15: [T2B-tbl, p2, C4B, C4F, p2, T2F-tbl] four times.

Rounds 16 - 18: [K-tbl, p3, k8, p3, k-tbl] four times.

Round 19: [T2F-tbl, p3, k6, p3, T2B-tbl] four times.

Round 20: P1, [k-tbl, p3, k6, p3, k-tbl, p2] three times, k-tbl, p3, k6, p3, k-tbl, p1.

Round 21: P1, [T2F-tbl, p3, k4, p3, T2B-tbl, p2] three times, T2F-tbl, p3, k4, p3, T2B-tbl, p1.

Round 22: P2, [k-tbl, p3, k4, p3, k-tbl, p4] three times, k-tbl, p3, k4, p3, k-tbl, p2.

Round 23: P2, [T2F-tbl, p3, k2, p3, T2B-tbl, p4] three times, T2F-tbl, p3, k2, p3, T2B-tbl, p2.

Round 24: P3, [k-tbl, p3, k2, p3, k-tbl, p6] three times, k-tbl, p3, k2, p3, k-tbl, p3.

Round 25: P3, [T2F-tbl, p6, T2B-tbl, p6] three times, T2F-tbl, p6, T2B-tbl, p3.

Round 26: P4, [k-tbl, p6, k-tbl, p8] three times, k-tbl, p6, k-tbl, p4.

Round 27: P4, [T2F-tbl, p4, T2B-tbl, p8] three times, T2F-tbl, p4, T2B-tbl, p2, k2.

Round 28: K2, [p3, k-tbl, p4, k-tbl, p3, k4] three times, p3, k-tbl, p4, k-tbl, p3, C4F using last two stitches of Round 28 and first two stitches of Round 29.

Round 29: [P3, T2F-tbl, p2, T2B-tbl, p3, C4F] three times, p3, T2F-tbl, p2, T2B-tbl, p3, k2.

Round 30: K2, [p4, k-tbl, p2, k-tbl, p4, k4] three times, p4, k-tbl, p2, k-tbl, p4, k2.

Round 31: [C4F, p2, T2F-tbl, T2B-tbl, p2, C4B] four times.

Round 32: K4, [p3, k-tbl twice, p3, k8] three times, p3, k-tbl twice, p3, k4.

Cuff

Round 1: K-tbl, *p2, k-tbl twice; repeat from * to last three stitches, p2, k-tbl.

Repeat Round 1 an additional seven times. Bind off all stitches using your favorite toe-up method. (I used the sewn bind-off.)

Sakura

I got the idea for these socks after Jennifer Jett of Woolgirl.com sent me a postcard of a lovely Japanese painting of cherry trees to use as inspiration for a design I was working on for her Woolgirl Sock Club. I ran a cherry tree motif up the back of the sock and nearly lost my mind working out the lace pattern for the instep. I finally managed to get it to look just how I wanted it and I couldn't be happier with the result. I hope you are as delighted by them as I am!

Materials:

Approximately 400 yards of fingering-weight yarn

Sample uses Curious Creek Wasonga (100% superwash merino wool) in Ruby Slipper.

US0 (2mm) needles or size needed to obtain gauge

Cable needle or locking stitch marker

Gauge:

9 stitches/12 rounds per inch in stockinette stitch

Size:

Foot circumference = approximately 8"

Toe

Using your favorite toe-up method, cast on eight instep stitches and eight heel stitches, dividing them over your selected needles. Place a marker at the start of the instep stitches to indicate the beginning of the round.

Round 1: K-fb, knit to last two instep stitches, k-fb, k1; repeat across heel stitches. 20 stitches.

Round 2: Knit.

Repeat Rounds 1 & 2 an additional 11 times. 64 stitches. Knit one round even.

Foot

Begin working the instep stitches in the *Petal Lace Pattern* from chart or written instructions on p. 125 while continuing to work the heel stitches in stockinette stitch.

Work until the foot from the tip of the toe to the needles measures approximately 5" less than the desired total length, ending with Round 10 of *Petal Lace Pattern*.

Petal Lace Pattern Chart

35	34	33	32	31	30	29	28	27	26	25	24	23	22	21	20	19	18	17	16	15	14	13	12	11	10	9	8	7	6	5	4	3	2	1	
•	C2B	C2F	•	λ	O	Λ	O				O	λ		░	░			λ	O	λ		λ	O	λ	O				O		•	C2B	C2F	•	10
•			•												░																•			•	9
•	C2B	C2F	•	λ	O	λ		λ	O		O	λ	O	λ	░			λ	O						O		O		O		•	C2B	C2F	•	8
•			•											░																	•			•	7
•	C2B	C2F	•		O					O	λ	O	Λ	O	λ			░	░	λ	O				O	Λ	O	λ	•	C2B	C2F	•	6
•			•													░	░												•			•	5
•	C2B	C2F	•		O			O	λ	O	λ		λ	O	λ		░	Λ	O	λ	O		O	λ		λ	O	λ	•	C2B	C2F	•	4
•			•																										•			•	3
•	C2B	C2F	•		O		O		O					O	λ		λ	O	Λ	O	λ	O						O	•	C2B	C2F	•	2
•			•										░	░																•			•	1

Legend:

- ☐ knit
- • purl
- O YO
- C2B - sl1 to cable needle and hold in back, k1, k1 from cable needle
- C2F - sl1 to cable needle and hold in front, k1, k1 from cable needle
- SSK
- k2tog
- SK2P
- S2KP
- k3tog
- ░ no stitch

Petal Lace Pattern:

(over 32 stitches and 10 rounds)

Round 1 *(and all odd-numbered rounds)***:** P1, k2, p1, knit to last four instep stitches, p1, k2, p1.

Round 2: P1, C2F, p1, k1, YO, k5, YO, SSK, YO, S2KP, YO, k2tog, k1, SSK, YO, k5, [YO, k1] three times, p1, C2B, p1. 35 stitches.

Round 4: P1, C2F, p1, SSK, YO, SSK, k1, k2tog, YO, k1, YO, SSK, YO, k3tog, k1, SSK, YO, SSK, k1, [k2tog, YO] twice, k3, YO, k1, p1, C2B, p1. 33 stitches.

Round 6: P1, C2F, p1, SSK, YO, S2KP, YO, k3, YO, SSK, k2, SSK, YO, S2KP, YO, k2tog, YO, k5, YO, k1, p1, C2B, p1. 32 stitches.

Round 8: P1, C2F, p1, [k1, YO] three times, k5, YO, k2tog, k1, SK2P, YO, k2tog, YO, k1, YO, SSK, k1, k2tog, YO, k2tog, p1, C2B, p1. 33 stitches.

Round 10: P1, C2F, p1, k1, YO, k3, [YO, SSK] twice, k1, k2tog, YO, k2tog, k2, k2tog, YO, k3, YO, S2KP, YO, k2tog, p1, C2B, p1. 32 stitches.

Heel

Gusset

Round 1: Work instep stitches in *Petal Lace Pattern* as established; k-fb in first heel stitch, knit to last two heel stitches, k-fb, k1.

Round 2: Continue working instep stitches in pattern; knit across heel stitches.

Repeat Rounds 1 & 2 an additional 19 times.

Turn Heel

Work across instep stitches in pattern. The heel turn will be worked back and forth on the 72 heel stitches.

Row 1 (RS): K51, W&T.
Row 2: P30, W&T.

Row 3: Knit to stitch before wrapped stitch (do not knit any wrapped stitches), W&T.
Row 4: Purl to stitch before wrapped stitch (do not purl any wrapped stitches), W&T.

Repeat Rows 3 & 4 an additional nine times - there are now 11 wrapped stitches on either side of ten unwrapped center stitches. Knit to end of heel stitches, lifting wraps RS as they are encountered, then work across instep stitches in *Petal Lace Pattern* as established.

Heel Flap

Work heel flap back and forth. The first set of instructions below are for the patterned heel flap as shown (see also *Cherry Tree Heel Flap* chart on p. 129). If you are working from the chart, you will need to first knit across the 20 gusset stitches before you'll reach the place on the heel needle where the chart begins (see Row 1 of written instructions below for the complete row).

If you would prefer not to have texture on your heel flap, skip to the second set of instructions for a reverse stockinette heel flap on p. 127.

Bobble: *To work the small bobbles on the back of Sakura's leg, first knit in front, back and front of same stitch (k-fbf). Turn to WS and purl across these three stitches. Turn back to WS and S2KP to eliminate the extra two stitches and form the bobble. If you have problems with little holes forming near your bobble, you can "choke" it by wrapping the working yarn around its base before moving on to the next stitch.*

Option 1 - Cherry Tree Heel Flap

Row 1 (RS): K51, lifting remaining wraps RS, SSK, turn.

Row 2: Sl1, k6, p1-tbl twice, k6, p2, k14, SSK, turn.

Row 3: Sl1, p14, C2B, p4, T3B-tbl, T2F-tbl, p2, bobble, p2, p2tog, turn.

Row 4: Sl1, k5, p-tbl, k3, p-tbl, k4, p2, k13, p-tbl, SSK, turn.

Row 5: Sl1, T2F-tbl, p12, C2B, p2, T3B-tbl, bobble, p2, T3F-tbl, p3, p2tog, turn.

Row 6: Sl1, k3, p-tbl, k7, p-tbl, k2, p2, k12, p-tbl, k1, SSK, turn.

Row 7: Sl1, p1, T2F-tbl, p11, C2B, p2, k-tbl, p5, bobble, p1, T2F-tbl, p1, bobble, p2tog, turn.

Row 8: Sl1, k2, p-tbl, k11, p2, k11, p-tbl, k2, SSK, turn.

Row 9: Sl1, p2, T3F-tbl, p9, C2B, p2, bobble, p8, k-tbl, p2, p2tog, turn.

Row 10: Sl1, k14, p2, k9, p-tbl, k4, SSK, turn.

Row 11: Sl1, p4, T3F-tbl, p2, bobble, p4, C2B, p11, bobble, p2, p2tog, turn.

Row 12: Sl1, k14, p2, k7, p-tbl twice, k5, SSK, turn.

Row 13: Sl1, p1, bobble, p2, T2B-tbl, T3F-tbl, p5, C2B, p14, p2tog, turn.

Row 14: Sl1, k11, p-tbl, k2, p2, k5, p-tbl, k3, p-tbl, k4, SSK, turn.

Row 15: Sl1, p2, T3B-tbl, p3, T3F-tbl, p1, bobble, p1, C2B, p2, T2F-tbl, p10, p2tog, turn.

Row 16: Sl1, k10, p-tbl, k3, p2, k3, p-tbl, k7, p-tbl, k2, SSK, turn.

Row 17: Sl1, p1, T2B-tbl, p1, bobble, p5, k-tbl, p3, C2B, p3, T2F-tbl, p9, p2tog, turn.

Row 18: Sl1, k9, p-tbl, k4, p2, k12, p-tbl, k1, SSK, turn.

Row 19: Sl1, p1, k-tbl, p8, bobble, p3, C2B, p4, T3F-tbl, p7, p2tog, turn.

Row 20: Sl1, k7, p-tbl, k6, p2, k14, SSK, turn.

Row 21: Sl1, p1, bobble, p12, C2B, p6, T3F-tbl, p2, bobble, p2, p2tog, turn.

Row 22: Sl1, k5, p-tbl twice, k7, p2, k14, SSK, turn.

Row 23: Sl1, p14, C2B, p3, bobble, p2, T2B-tbl, T3F-tbl, p3, p2tog, turn.

Row 24: Sl1, [k3, p-tbl] twice, k6, p2, k2, p-tbl, k11, SSK, turn.

Row 25: Sl1, p10, T2B-tbl, p2, C2B, p4, T3B-tbl, p3, T3F-tbl, p1, p2tog, turn.

Row 26: Sl1, k1, p-tbl, k7, p-tbl, k4, p2, k3, p-tbl, k10, SSK, turn.

Row 27: Sl1, p9, T2B-tbl, p3, C2B, p1, bobble, p1, T2B-tbl, p1, bobble, p5, k-tbl, p1, p2tog, turn.

Row 28: Sl1, k10, p-tbl, k3, p2, k4, p-tbl, k9, SSK, turn.

Row 29: Sl1, p7, T3B-tbl, p4, C2B, p3, k-tbl, p8, bobble, p1, p2tog, turn.

Row 30: Sl1, k14, p2, k6, p-tbl, k7, SSK, turn.

Row 31: Sl1, p2, bobble, p2, T3B-tbl, p6, C2B, p3, bobble, p10, p2tog, turn.

Row 32: Sl1, k14, p2, k7, p-tbl twice, k5, SSK, turn.

Row 33: Sl1, p3, T3B-tbl, T2F-tbl, p2, bobble, p3, C2B, p14, p2tog, turn.

Row 34: Sl1, k1, p-tbl, k12, p2, k6, p-tbl, k3, p-tbl, k3, SSK, turn.

Row 35: Sl1, p1, T3B-tbl, bobble, p2, T3F-tbl, p4, C2B, p11, T2B-tbl, p1, p2tog, turn.

Row 36: Sl1, k2, p-tbl, k11, p2, k4, p-tbl, k7, p-tbl, k1, SSK, turn.

Row 37: Sl1, p1, k-tbl, p5, bobble, p1, T2F-tbl, p1, bobble, p1, C2B, p10, T2B-tbl, p2, p2tog, turn.

Row 38: Sl1, k3, p-tbl, k10, p2, k3, p-tbl, k10, SSK, turn.

Row 39: Sl1, p1, bobble, p8, k-tbl, p3, C2B, p8, T3B-tbl, p3, p2tog, do not turn (one gusset stitch remains on right-hand edge of heel).

Round 40: Work across instep stitches in *Petal Lace Pattern* as established; p2tog, p14, k2, p8, k-tbl, p6. 32 heel stitches.

Option 2 - Reverse Stockinette Heel Flap

Row 1 (RS): K51, lifting remaining wraps RS, SSK, turn.

Row 2: Sl1, k30, SSK, turn.

Row 3: Sl1, p30, p2tog, turn.

Repeat Rows 2 & 3 an additional 18 times. Do not turn after working final repeat of Row 3 (one gusset stitch remains on right-hand edge of heel).

Next Round: Work across the instep stitches in Petal Lace Pattern as established; p2tog, p14, k2, p8, k-tbl, p6. 32 heel stitches.

Leg

Continuing in the round, work the instep stitches in *Petal Lace Pattern* as established and the heel stitches in the *Cherry Tree Pattern* from the chart on p. 130 or written instructions below. End with Round 20 or 40 of the *Cherry Tree Pattern* when leg measures approximately 7" from the bottom (Row 1) of the heel or $^1/_2$" less than desired finished length.

Cherry Tree Pattern:
(over 32 stitches and 40 rounds)

Round 1: P11, bobble, p3, C2B, p3, bobble, p2, T3B-tbl, p6.

Round 2: P15, k2, p6, k-tbl twice, p7.

Round 3: P15, C2B, p4, T3B-tbl, T2F-tbl, p2, bobble, p3.

Round 4: P1, k-tbl, p13, k2, p4, k-tbl, p3, k-tbl, p6.

Round 5: P1, T2F-tbl, p12, C2B, p2, T3B-tbl, bobble, p2, T3F-tbl, p4.

Round 6: P2, k-tbl, p12, k2, p2, k-tbl, p7, k-tbl, p4.

Round 7: P2, T2F-tbl, p11, C2B, p2, k-tbl, p5, bobble, p1, T2F-tbl, p1, bobble, p1.

Round 8: P3, k-tbl, p11, k2, p11, k-tbl, p3.

Round 9: P3, T3F-tbl, p9, C2B, p2, bobble, p8, k-tbl, p3.

Round 10: P5, k-tbl, p9, k2, p15.

Round 11: P5, T3F-tbl, p2, bobble, p4, C2B, p11, bobble, p3.

Round 12: P6, k-tbl twice, p7, k2, p15.

Round 13: P2, bobble, p2, T2B-tbl, T3F-tbl, p5, C2B, p15.

Round 14: P5, k-tbl, p3, k-tbl, p5, k2, p2, k-tbl, p12.

Round 15: P3, T3B-tbl, p3, T3F-tbl, p1, bobble, p1, C2B, p2, T2F-tbl, p11.

Round 16: P3, k-tbl, p7, k-tbl, p3, k2, p3, k-tbl, p11.

Round 17: Bobble, p1, T2B-tbl, p1, bobble, p5, k-tbl, p3, C2B, p3, T2F-tbl, p10.

Round 18: P2, k-tbl, p12, k2, p4, k-tbl, p10.

Round 19: P2, k-tbl, p8, bobble, p3, C2B, p4, T3F-tbl, p8.

Round 20: P15, k2, p6, k-tbl, p8.

Round 21: P2, bobble, p12, C2B, p6, T3F-tbl, p2, bobble, p3.

Round 22: P15, k2, p7, k-tbl twice, p6.

Round 23: P15, C2B, p3, bobble, p2, T2B-tbl, T3F-tbl, p4.

Round 24: P12, k-tbl, p2, k2, p6, k-tbl, p3, k-tbl, p4.

Round 25: P11, T2B-tbl, p2, C2B, p4, T3B-tbl, p3, T3F-tbl, p1, bobble.

Round 26: P11, k-tbl, p3, k2, p4, k-tbl, p7, k-tbl, p2.

Round 27: P10, T2B-tbl, p3, C2B, p1, bobble, p1, T2B-tbl, p1, bobble, p5, k-tbl, p2.

Round 28: P10, k-tbl, p4, k2, p3, k-tbl, p11.

Round 29: P8, T3B-tbl, p4, C2B, p3, k-tbl, p8, bobble, p2.

Round 30: P8, k-tbl, p6, k2, p15.

Round 31: P3, bobble, p2, T3B-tbl, p6, C2B, p3, bobble, p11.

Round 32: P6, k-tbl twice, p7, k2, p15.

Round 33: P4, T3B-tbl, T2F-tbl, p2, bobble, p3, C2B, p15.

Round 34: P4, k-tbl, p3, k-tbl, p6, k2, p12, k-tbl, p2.

Round 35: P2, T3B-tbl, bobble, p2, T3F-tbl, p4, C2B, p11, T2B-tbl, p2.

Round 36: P2, k-tbl, p7, k-tbl, p4, k2, p11, k-tbl, p3.

Round 37: P2, k-tbl, p5, bobble, p1, T2F-tbl, p1, bobble, p1, C2B, p10, T2B-tbl, p3.

Round 38: P11, k-tbl, p3, k2, p10, k-tbl, p4.

Round 39: P2, bobble, p8, k-tbl, p3, C2B, p8, T3B-tbl, p4.

Round 40: P15, k2, p8, k-tbl, p6.

Cuff

Round 1: Purl.

Round 2: Knit.

Round 3: Purl.

Bind off all sts using your favorite toe-up method. (I used the yarn over bind-off.)

Note: If you find that the garter stitch edging is too loose to fit your calf well, work the following rounds instead of Cuff Rounds 1-3.

Round 1: P1, C2F, [p1, k2] four times, p1, k3, [p1, k2] four times, p1, C2B, p1; k2, p1, [C2B, p1] nine times, k2.

Round 2: [P1, k2] five times, p1, k3, [p1, k2] five times, p1; [k2, p1] 10 times, k2.

Repeat Rounds 1 & 2 an additional four times before binding off.

Cherry Tree Heel Flap Chart

	knit on RS, purl on WS		k-tbl on RS, p-tbl on WS
	purl on RS, knit on WS		C2B - sl1 to cable needle and hold in back, k1, k1 from cable needle
	SSK (both RS and WS)		T2F-tbl - sl1 to cable needle and hold in front, p1, k-tbl from cable needle
	p2tog (both RS and WS)		T2B-tbl - sl1 to cable needle and hold in back, k-tbl, p1 from cable needle
	sl1		T3F-tbl - sl1 to cable needle and hold in front, p2, k-tbl from cable needle
	bobble		T3B-tbl - sl2 to cable needle and hold in back, k-tbl, p2 from cable needle

Cherry Tree Pattern Chart

Toe-Up!

Chapter 8
Blank Worksheets

In this chapter you will find blank versions of the worksheets we explored in Chapters 3 and 4. Use the examples in those chapters if you need help filling them out. I recommend starting a file of filled-out worksheets with notes as to what fit particularly well and what didn't. When you start a new sock, you can look through this file and see if you've already got the perfect toe or heel to use.

Toe Worksheets

Heel Worksheets

Non-Shaped Round Toe Worksheet

Numbers Needed:

A _____ = half the number of stitches to cast on, generally about $\frac{1}{8}$ of the total number of stitches needed for foot

B _____ = half the number of stitches needed for foot (this assumes that the foot has an equal number of instep and heel stitches - if not, see checks #1 and #2 in "Check That" section)

C _____ = number of stitches to increase on each half of sock, (B - A)

D _____ = number of increase rounds, (C ÷ 2)

Check That:

1. If B is not a whole number because the number of stitches needed for the foot is odd, round it down to the nearest whole number. On the last round of the toe, increase one stitch in the join between the instep and heel stitches and place it on the correct needle.

2. If B is a whole number, but the number of instep stitches does not equal the heel stitches, set B equal to whichever is smaller. When you are done with the toe increases, determine how many stitches still need to be added and to which side of the sock (instep or heel). Distribute them evenly around the final round of the toe.

3. (B - A) is a multiple of two. If it's not, increase or decrease A by one.

To Work:

Cast on (2 x A) _____ stitches, dividing them evenly across two circulars or four dpns.

Round 1: Knit.

Round 2: K-fb, knit to last two instep stitches, k-fb, k1; repeat across heel stitches. Four stitches increased.

Repeat Rounds 1-2 an additional (D - 1) _____ times. There are now (B x 2) _____ stitches on the needles (if needed, insert any additional increases in the next round). Knit one round even.

Shaped Round Toe Worksheet

Numbers Needed:

A _____ = half the number of stitches to cast on, generally about $\frac{1}{8}$ of the total number of stitches needed for foot

B _____ = half the number of stitches needed for foot (this assumes that the foot has an equal number of instep and heel stitches - if not, see checks #1 and #2 in "Check That" section)

C _____ = number of stitches to increase on each half of sock, (B - A)

D _____ = number of increase rounds, (C ÷ 2)

E _____ = D ÷ 3, rounded to the nearest whole number

Check That:

1. If B is not a whole number because the number of stitches needed for the foot is odd, round it down to the nearest whole number. On the last round of the toe, increase one stitch in the join between the instep and heel stitches and place it on the correct needle.

2. If B is a whole number, but the number of instep stitches does not equal the heel stitches, set B equal to whichever is smaller. When you are done with the toe increases, determine how many stitches still need to be added and to which side of the sock (instep or heel). Distribute them evenly around the final round of the toe.

3. (B - A) is a multiple of two. If it's not, increase or decrease A by one.

To Work:

Cast on (2 x A) ____ stitches, dividing them evenly across two circulars or four dpns.

Round 1: K-fb, knit to last two instep stitches, k-fb, k1; repeat across heel stitches. Four stitches increased.

Repeat Round 1 an additional (E - 1) _____ times. There are now [(E x 4) + (A x 2)] ____ stitches on the needles.

Next Round: Knit.

Next Round: K-fb, knit to last two instep stitches, k-fb, k1; repeat across heel stitches. Four stitches increased.

Repeat last two rounds an additional (D - E - 1) ____ times. There are now (B x 2) ____ stitches on the needles (if needed, insert any additional increases in the next round). Knit one round even.

Anatomical Round Toe Worksheet

Numbers Needed:

A _____ = half the number of stitches to cast on, generally about $1/8$ of the total number of stitches needed for foot

B _____ = half the number of stitches needed for foot (this assumes that the foot has an equal number of instep and heel stitches - if not, see checks #1 and #2 in "Check That" section)

C _____ = number of stitches to increase on each half of sock, (B - A)

D _____ = number of outer edge increases, [(C ÷ 3) x 2], rounded to the nearest whole number

E _____ = number of inner edge increases, (C - D)

Check That:

1. If B is not a whole number because the number of stitches needed for the foot is odd, round it down to the nearest whole number. On the last round of the toe, increase one stitch in the join between the instep and heel stitches and place it on the correct needle.

2. If B is a whole number, but the number of instep stitches does not equal the heel stitches, set B equal to whichever is smaller. When you are done with the toe increases, determine how many stitches still need to be added and to which side of the sock (instep or heel). Distribute them evenly around the final round of the toe.

3. (B - A) is a multiple of two. If it's not, increase or decrease A by one.

To Work:

Cast on (2 x A) _____ stitches, dividing them evenly across two circulars or four dpns.

Round I: K-fb, knit to last two instep stitches, k-fb, k1; repeat across heel stitches. Four stitches increased.

Repeat Round 1 an additional (E - 1) _____ times. There are now [(E x 4) + (A x 2)] _____ stitches on the needles.

Continued on next page...

Anatomical Round Toe Worksheet - p2

Left Sock Only

Next Round: Knit.

Next Round: K-fb, knit to end of instep stitches; knit to last two heel stitches, k-fb, k1. Two stitches increased.

Repeat last two rounds an additional (D - E - 1) _____ times. There are now (B x 2) _____ stitches on the needles (if needed, insert any additional increases in the next round). Knit one round even.

Right Sock Only

Next Round: Knit.

Next Round: Knit to last two instep stitches, k-fb, k1; k1, k-fb, knit to end of heel stitches. Two stitches increased.

Repeat last two rounds an additional (D - E - 1) _____ times. There are now (B x 2) _____ stitches on the needles (if needed, insert any additional increases in the next round). Knit one round even.

❖ ❖ ❖

Star Toe Worksheet

Numbers Needed:

A ____ = number of stitches needed for foot

B ____ = number of stitches to increase, (A - 16)

C ____ = number of full increase rounds, (B ÷ 4), rounded down to the nearest whole number

D ____ = leftover increases, [B - (C x 4)]

To Work:

Cast on six stitches, three on each of two circulars or dpns, leaving a 16" tail. Knit each stitch with both the working yarn and the tail, ending with 12 loops on the needles. Each of these loops will be knitted as a separate stitch on the first round of the toe.

If working on dpns, divide these stitches evenly across four dpns with three stitches on each needle. If working on circulars, place a marker in the center of each needle, dividing the stitches into groups of three.

Round 1: Knit.

Round 2: *K-fb, k2; repeat from * to end of round. 16 stitches.

Round 3: Knit.

Round 4: *K-fb, knit to marker; repeat from * to end of round. Four stitches increased.

Repeat Rounds 3 - 4 an additional (C - 1) ____ times. There are now [(C x 4) + 16] ____ stitches on the needles. Knit one round even.

If D is not 0, work one more increase round, spacing the leftover increases as follows:

- *1 leftover increase:* Place increase after 2nd or 4th marker.
- *2 leftover increases:* Place increases after 1st and 3rd markers.
- *3 leftover increases:* Place increases after 1st, 2nd and 3rd markers or 1st, 3rd and 4th markers.

Short-Row Toe Worksheet

Numbers Needed:

A ____ = half the number of stitches needed for foot

B ____ = A ÷ 3

C ____ = wrapped side stitches, B if B is a whole number, or adjust up or down according to check #1 in "Check That" section

D ____ = unwrapped center stitches, B if B is a whole number, or adjust up or down according to check #1 in "Check That" section

Check That:

1. Ensure that $[(2 \times C) + D] = A$. Adjust C and D by a stitch in either direction to get the formula to work. Your goal is to get an equal number of wrapped stitches (C) on either side of the unwrapped center stitches (D), i.e. if A = 30, C and D both equal 10; if A = 32, C = 11 and D = 10.

2. If you have a narrow toe footprint, decrease D and increase C. If you have a wide toe footprint, increase D and decrease C, always making sure the formula above totals up.

To Work:

Cast on A ____ stitches on each of two circulars or dpns or (A x 2) ____ stitches total. The first (instep) needle holds the toe stitches, which are worked back and forth until the toe is complete. The stitches on the second (heel) needle are held until it is time to work the foot.

Shape Bottom of Toe

Row 1 (RS): Knit to last stitch on first needle, W&T (see glossary).

Row 2 (WS): Purl to last stitch on first needle, W&T.

Row 3: Knit to the stitch before the first wrapped stitch you come to, W&T.

Row 4: Purl to the stitch before the first wrapped stitch you come to, W&T.

Repeat the previous two rows until C ____ stitches are wrapped on either side of D ____ unwrapped center stitches.

Continued on next page...

Short-Row Toe Worksheet - p2

Shape Top of Toe

Row 1 (RS): Knit to first wrapped stitch (do not knit across any wrapped stitches), lift wrap RS, turn.

Row 2 (WS): Sl1, purl to first wrapped stitch (do not purl across any wrapped stitches), lift wrap WS, turn.

Row 3: Sl1, knit to next wrapped stitch (just past the stitch unwrapped on the previous RS row), lift wrap RS, turn.

Row 4: Sl1, purl to next wrapped stitch (just past the stitch unwrapped on the previous WS row), lift wrap WS, turn.

Repeat the previous two rows an additional (C - 3) _____ times until a single wrapped stitch remains on either side.

Next Round: Sl1, knit to last wrapped stitch, lift wrap RS, but do not turn. If working on dpns, divide the stitches evenly across four dpns. Knit across the heel stitches to complete the round.

Next Round: Lift the final wrap (which is at the beginning of the instep needle) RS, then knit the rest of the round even.

Toe-Up!

Short-Row Heel Worksheet

Numbers Needed:

A _____ = heel stitches, generally half of the total number of sock stitches

B _____ = A ÷ 3

C _____ = wrapped side stitches, B if B is a whole number, or adjust up or down according to check #1 in "Check That" section

D _____ = unwrapped center stitches, B if B is a whole number, or adjust up or down according to check #1 in "Check That" section

E _____ = heel length in inches, (C x 2 ÷ rows per inch), rounded up to nearest $^1/_4$"

Check That:

1. Ensure that [(2 x C) + D = A]. Adjust C and D by a stitch in either direction to get the formula to work. Your goal is to get an equal number of wrapped stitches (C) on either side of the unwrapped center stitches (D), i.e. if A = 30, C and D both equal 10; if A = 32, C = 11 and D = 10.

2. If you have a narrow heel, decrease D and increase C. If you have a wide heel, increase D and decrease C, always making sure the formula in check #1 totals up.

To Work:

Start heel when foot measures E ____ less than desired finished length from tip of toe. Place A ____ stitches on a single needle (the heel needle) and begin working back and forth across these stitches.

Shape Bottom of Heel

Row 1 (RS): Knit to last stitch on first needle, W&T.

Row 2 (WS): Purl to last stitch on first needle, W&T.

Row 3: Knit to the stitch before the first wrapped stitch you come to, W&T.

Row 4: Purl to the stitch before the first wrapped stitch you come to, W&T.

Repeat the previous two rows until C _____ stitches are wrapped on either side of D ____ unwrapped center stitches.

Continued on next page...

Short-Row Heel Worksheet - p2

Shape Top of Heel

Row 1 (RS): Knit to first wrapped stitch (do not knit across any wrapped stitches), lift wrap RS (see glossary), turn.

Row 2 (WS): Sl1, purl to first wrapped stitch (do not purl across any wrapped stitches), lift wrap WS, turn.

Row 3: Sl1, knit to next wrapped stitch (just past the stitch unwrapped on the previous RS row), lift wrap RS, turn.

Row 4: Sl1, purl to next wrapped stitch (just past the stitch unwrapped on the previous WS row), lift wrap WS, turn.

Repeat the previous two rows an additional (C - 3) _____ times until a single wrapped stitch remains on either side.

Next Row: Sl1, knit to last wrapped stitch, lift wrap RS, but do not turn - you will be at the start of the instep stitches. If working on dpns, re-divide the heel stitches across two dpns.

Next Round: Work across the instep stitches in pattern; lift the final wrap (which is at the beginning of the heel needle) RS, then knit across the remaining heel stitches.

Hybrid Heel Worksheet

Numbers Needed:

A _____ = heel stitches, generally half of the total number of sock stitches

B _____ = A ÷ 3

C _____ = wrapped side stitches, B if B is a whole number, or adjust up or down according to check #1 in "Check That" section

D _____ = unwrapped center stitches, B if B is a whole number, or adjust up or down according to check #1 in "Check That" section

E _____ = gusset stitches, (A ÷ 2), rounded up if not a whole number

F _____ = heel length in inches, ([(E x 2) + (C x 2)] ÷ rows per inch), rounded up to nearest $\frac{1}{4}$"

Check That:

1. Ensure that [(2 x C) + D] = A. Adjust C and D by a stitch in either direction to get the formula to work. Your goal is to get an equal number of wrapped stitches (C) on either side of the unwrapped center stitches (D), i.e. if A = 30, C and D both equal 10; if A = 32, C = 11 and D = 10.

2. If you have a narrow heel, decrease D and increase C. If you have a wide heel, increase D and decrease C, always making sure the formula in check #1 totals up.

3. If you have a high instep or you're having trouble fitting a sock over your heel, increase E by 1 to 4 stitches.

To Work:

Gusset

Start gusset when foot measures F _____ less than desired finished length from tip of toe.

Round 1: Work across instep stitches in pattern; k-fb, knit to last 2 heel stitches, k-fb, k1.

Round 2: Work across instep stitches in pattern; knit heel stitches.

Repeat Rounds 1-2 an additional (E - 2) _____ times, then work Round 1 once more. You will now have [(2 x E) + A] _____ heel stitches. Place a stitch marker on each side of the heel to separate the gusset stitches from the center heel stitches (the gusset markers will be E _____ stitches from either side of the heel).

Continued on next page...

Hybrid Heel Worksheet - p2

Shape Bottom of Heel

Row 1 (RS): Knit to stitch before the 2nd gusset marker ([A + E - 1] _____ stitches), W&T.

Row 2 (WS): Purl to stitch before the 1st gusset marker ([A - 2] ____ stitches), W&T.

Row 3: Knit to the stitch before the first wrapped stitch you come to, W&T.

Row 4: Purl to the stitch before the first wrapped stitch you come to, W&T.

Repeat the previous two rows until C _____ stitches are wrapped on either side of D ____ unwrapped center stitches.

Next Round: With RS facing, knit to end of heel stitches, lifting wraps RS as you encounter them, then work across instep stitches in pattern to bring you back to the start of the heel.

Work Heel Flap

Row 1 (RS): Knit E ____ stitches, then knit (A - 1) _____ lifting remaining wraps RS as you encounter them. You should now be one stitch before the second gusset marker. Remove marker and SSK the stitches that were on either side of the marker, turn.

Row 2 (WS): [Sl1, p1] to stitch before marker (if A is an even number then end with sl1, otherwise end with p1). You should now be one stitch before the first gusset marker. Remove marker and p2tog the stitches that were on either side of the marker, turn.

Row 3: Sl1, knit (A - 2) ____, SSK, turn.

Row 4: [Sl1, p1] to stitch before gap formed by previous WS row's turn (if A is an even number then end with sl1, otherwise end with p1), p2tog, turn.

Repeat the previous two rows an additional (E - 3) ____ times, then work Row 3 once more, but do not turn - you will be slowly working up the edge of the gusset and forming the heel flap as you go.

Next Round: Work across instep stitches in pattern; k2tog, knit to end of heel.

Afterthought Heel Worksheet

Numbers Needed:

A ____ = number of heel stitches; generally half of the total number of sock stitches

B ____ = total stitches after waste yarn is removed, [(A + 1) x 2]

C ____ = A ÷ 2

D ____ = heel length in inches, ([(B ÷ 2) - (C ÷ 2)] ÷ rows per inch), rounded up to nearest $^1/_4$"

To Work:

When foot measures approximately D ____ less than desired finished length from tip of toe, pick up a piece of scrap/waste yarn and use it to knit across the heel stitches. Then, drop the waste yarn, go back to the start of the heel, pick up the working yarn and knit across the waste yarn stitches. Continue knitting the leg of your sock with the working yarn - the waste yarn holds the stitches where the heel will eventually go.

When it's time to make your heel, go back and carefully pick up the stitches held by the waste yarn across the top and bottom of the heel. There will be an extra stitch on the top needle. Pick up one more stitch in a corner of the heel with the bottom needle so that there is an equal number of stitches on both needles or B ____ total.

Place a marker at each side of the heel to indicate where the heel cup decreases will go (|| indicates the location of the marker in the following instructions).

Join yarn to be used for heel in either corner.

Round 1: Knit.

Round 2: K1, SSK, knit to 3 stitches before first side marker, k2tog, k1 || k1, SSK, knit to 3 stitches before second side marker, k2tog, k1 ||.

Repeat these two rounds until there are C ____ or fewer stitches left or until the heel is about D ____ deep.

Place the stitches between each marker on a single needle (i.e. top-of-heel stitches on one needle, bottom-of-heel stitches on another) and graft the heel cup closed using Kitchener Stitch.

Star Heel Worksheet

Numbers Needed:

A _____ = number of heel stitches; generally half of the total number of sock stitches

B _____ = total stitches after waste yarn is removed, $[(A + 1) \times 2]$

C _____ = A ÷ 2

D _____ = heel length in inches, $([(B ÷ 2) - (C ÷ 2)] ÷ \text{rows per inch})$, rounded up to nearest $1/4$"

Check That:

1. B is divisible by 4. If needed, pick up extra stitches in the corners where the heel meets the instep.

To Work:

When foot measures approximately D _____ less than desired finished length from tip of toe, pick up a piece of scrap/waste yarn and use it to knit across the heel stitches. Then, drop the waste yarn, go back to the start of the heel, pick up the working yarn and knit across the waste yarn stitches. Continue knitting the leg of your sock with the working yarn - the waste yarn holds the stitches where the heel will eventually go.

When it's time to make your heel, go back and carefully pick up the stitches held by the waste yarn across the top and bottom of the heel. There will be an extra stitch on the top needle. Pick up one more stitch in a corner of the heel with the bottom needle so that there is an equal number of stitches on both needles or B _____ total. Place markers every (B ÷ 4) _____ stitches.

Join yarn to be used for heel.
Round 1: Knit.
Round 2: *Knit to 2 stitches before marker, k2tog; repeat from * an additional 3 times.

Repeat these two rounds until there are C _____ or fewer stitches left or until the heel is about D _____ deep.

Place the stitches between each marker on a single needle (i.e. top-of-heel stitches on one needle, bottom-of-heel stitches on another) and graft the heel cup closed using Kitchener Stitch.

Abbreviations

These are the standard abbreviations used throughout the text. See the *Glossary of Techniques* for more detailed info on and photo tutorials of the more complicated of these procedures.

‖: Slip marker

C2B: Slip one stitch to cable needle and hold in back, k1, k1 from cable needle

C2F: Slip one stitch to cable needle and hold in front, k1, k1 from cable needle

C3B: Slip two stitches to cable needle and hold in back, k1, k2 from cable needle

C3F: Slip one stitch to cable needle and hold in front, k2, k1 from cable needle

C4B: Slip two stitches to cable needle and hold in back, k2, k2 from cable needle

C4F: Slip two stitches to cable needle and hold in front, k2, k2 from cable needle

CC: Contrasting color

dpn: Double-pointed needle

k: Knit

k2tog: Knit two stitches together

k2tog-tbl: Knit two stitches together through back loops

k3tog: Knit three stitches together

k-fb: Knit in front and back of stitch

k-tbl: Knit stitch through back loop

m1: Increase one stitch by lifting bar between needles and knitting it through the back loop

m1-pwise: Increase one stitch by lifting bar between needles and purling it through the back loop

MC: Main color

p: Purl

p2tog: Purl two stitches together

p-tbl: Purl stitch through back loop

RS: Right side

S2KP: Slip two stitches together as if to knit, k1, pass slipped stitches over knitted stitch

SK2P: Slip one stitch as if to knit, k2tog, pass slipped stitch over k2tog

sl: Slip stitch as if to purl

SSK: Slip next two stitches one at a time as if to knit, insert left needle tip into front of stitches and knit them together

T2B-tbl: Slip one stitch to cable needle and hold in back, k-tbl, p1 from cable needle

T2F-tbl: Slip one stitch to cable needle and hold in front, p1, k-tbl from cable needle

T3B: Slip two stitches to cable needle and hold in back, k1, p2 from cable needle

T3F: Slip one stitch to cable needle and hold in front, p2, k1 from cable needle

T3B-tbl: Slip two stitches to cable needle and hold in back, k-tbl, p2 from cable needle

T3F-tbl: Slip one stitch to cable needle and hold in front, p2, k-tbl from cable needle

W&T: Wrap and turn

WS: Wrong side

YO: Yarn over

Glossary of Techniques

Crochet Chain: To crochet a chain, start with a slip knot on your crochet hook. Then, wrap the yarn around the hook and pull through.

k-fb: Knit in front and back of the same stitch. This increases your stitch count by one.

Kitchener Stitch: To prepare stitches for Kitchener Stitch, place half of the stitches on one needle and half on the other with the needles parallel to where the seam will ultimately be.

Cut the yarn leaving a 12" - 16" tail. Thread the tail on a yarn needle and position the needles so that the tips are pointing right and the yarn tail is in back.

Step 1: Insert yarn needle into first stitch on front needle as if to purl and pull through, leaving stitch on needle.

Step 2: Insert yarn needle into first stitch on back needle as if to knit and pull through, leaving stitch on needle.

Step 3: Insert yarn needle into first stitch on front needle as if to knit and pull through, slipping stitch off needle.

Step 4: Insert yarn needle into next stitch on front needle as if to purl and pull through, leaving stitch on needle.

Step 5: Insert yarn needle into first stitch on back needle as if to purl and pull through, slipping stitch off needle.

Step 6: Insert yarn needle into next stitch on back needle as if to knit and pull through, leaving stitch on needle.

Repeat Steps 3 - 6 until a single stitch remains on each needle, then work Steps 3 and 5 to complete the seam. Thread yarn tail to WS of work and weave in end to finish seam.

Knitting/Purling Through Back Loop: To work a stitch through the back loop, insert the needle through the leg of the stitch that is in back of the needle instead of the front leg through which it is usually worked. This results in a twisted stitch.

Here's how to insert the needle to knit through the back loop:

Here's how to insert the needle to purl through the back loop:

Knit the wrap and its corresponding stitch together through their back loops.

Lift Wrap RS: Lifting wraps hides them and completes the short-row process. To lift a wrap on a RS row or round, use the tip of the right needle to pick up the wrap from the front side and lift it onto the left needle next to the stitch around which it was wrapped.

Toe-Up!

Lift Wrap WS: To lift a wrap on a WS row, use the tip of the right needle to pick up the wrap from the back side (RS of work) and lift it onto the left needle to the left of the stitch around which it was wrapped.

You may be able to get a good result by simply purling the stitch and the wrap together. If you find, however, that the sides of your heel are looking significantly different, try a SSP with the wrap and the stitch (slip the stitch as if to knit, then slip the wrap as if to knit, slip them both back onto the left needle and purl them together) to make it more symmetrical.

m1/m1-pwise: To increase using the m1 or "make one" method, lift the bar between the needles with the right needle tip, inserting it from back to front.

Place the bar on the left needle and knit it through the back loop.

To increase using the m1-pwise method, lift the bar between the needles with the right needle tip, inserting it from back to front.

Place the bar on the left needle and purl it through the back loop.

Pick Up Stitch: To pick up a stitch, insert the tip of the right needle into the knitting from RS to WS in the spot where you need the extra stitch.

Wrap the yarn around the needle as if you are knitting and pull up a loop.

For the purposes of this book, you'll really only need to pick up stitches in the corner of the afterthought heel.

Provisional Cast-On: With a length of smooth, contrasting-color waste yarn, crochet a chain that is four or five stitches longer than the number of stitches you need to cast on. With your empty needle, pick up a stitch in the back loop of each chain starting a few chains from the end.

When it is time to remove the provisional cast on, carefully undo the chain and place the live stitches on your needle.

Slip As If To Knit/As If To Purl: In my classes, I often run into questions as to why stitches are slipped as if to knit versus as if to purl in certain situations. The rule of thumb is that, unless the instructions specify otherwise, stitches are always slipped as if to purl so that they are not twisted when moving from needle to needle. The exception is for decreases, such as SSK, S2KP or SK2P which require the stitches to be slipped as if to knit so that the stitch that lies on top of the decrease is not twisted.

To slip a stitch as if to knit: Insert the right needle into the first stitch on the left needle as if you were going to knit it, but instead slip it onto the right needle.

To slip a stitch as if to purl: Insert the right needle into the first stitch on the left needle as if you were going to purl it, but instead slip it onto the right needle. I also call this the "tip to tip" method since you slip the stitch across with the needle tips pointing directly at each other.

Slip Knot: To place a slip knot on the needle, make a circle with the yarn tail and pull the strand that goes to the yarn ball through the center. Place this loop on the needle and tighten. When you pull the loop off the needle and tug the tail, the knot should pop right out.

Wrap on RS of work: Leaving yarn in back, slip next stitch to right needle. Bring yarn between needles to front of work. Slip stitch back to left needle wrapping the yarn around the base of the stitch. Bring the yarn to the back of the work between the needles to complete the wrap. Turn the work to begin working across the WS.

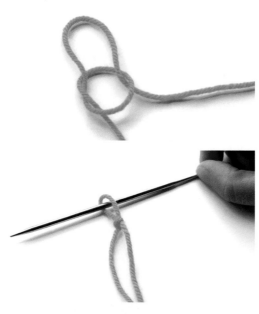

Stockinette Stitch: This term is commonly used to refer to smooth knitted fabric. When working in the round, knit every round to produce stockinette. When working flat, knit the right side rows and purl the wrong side rows.

W&T: Wrap and turn is a technique used in short-row heel and toe shaping to help prevent holes in the sides of the heel. There are a number of different methods of wrapping and turning - this is the one I use for my socks. Unless otherwise indicated, all stitches should be slipped as if to purl (without twisting).

Wrap on WS of work: Leaving yarn in front, slip next stitch to right needle. Bring yarn between needles to back of work. Slip stitch back to left needle wrapping the yarn around the base of the stitch. Bring the yarn to the front of the work between the needles to complete the wrap. Turn the work to begin working across the RS.

Wrapping Yarn Twice: For the *Gull Wing* stitch pattern, you'll need to wrap the yarn twice when you are knitting it in order to create an extra long stitch. To do this, work the stitch as if you are going to knit it normally, but instead of pulling the yarn through when it's wrapped only once, wrap it again so that you're pulling two loops through the stitch being knitted.

Yarn Over: To work a yarn over, bring the yarn between the needle tips to the front of the work, and then over the top of the right-hand needle to the back of the work. If you're knitting the next stitch, leave the yarn in back of the needle and work the next stitch.

If you're purling the next stitch, you'll bring the yarn completely around the needle and back to the front of the work to purl the next stitch.

Resources

Yarn

Blue Moon Fiber Arts
http://www.bluemoonfiberarts.com

Brown Sheep
http://www.brownsheep.com

Buffalo Gold
http://www.buffalogold.net

Cascade Yarns
http://www.cascadeyarns.com

Classic Elite
http://www.classiceliteyarns.com

Crystal Palace Yarns
http://www.straw.com

Curious Creek Fibers
http://www.curiouscreek.com

Dale of Norway
http://www. daleofnorway.com/dalegarn

Debbie Bliss/KFI
http://www.knittingfever.com

Dream In Color
http://www.dreamincoloryarn.com

Fleece Artist
http://www.fleeceartist.com

Lavender Sheep
http://www.lavendersheep.com

Lorna's Laces
http://www.lornaslaces.net

Louet North America
http://www.louet.com

Mountain Colors
http://www.mountaincolors.com

Nature's Palette
http://www.handjiveknits.com/

ShibuiKnits
http://www.shibuiknits.com

SWTC
http://www.soysilk.com

Needles

Crystal Palace
http://www.straw.com

Skacel Knitting
http://www.skacelknitting.com

Notions

Clover Needlecraft, Inc.
http://www.clover-usa.com

Fiber Trends
http://www.fibertrends.com

Susan Bates
http://www.coatsandclark.com

Books

Bordhi, Cat. *Socks Soar on Two Circular Needles*. Passing Paws Press, 2001.

Bordhi, Cat. *New Pathways for Sock Knitters: Book One*. Passing Paws Press, 2007.

Bush, Nancy. *Knitting Vintage Socks*. Interweave Press, 2005.

Galeskas, Bev. *The Magic Loop: Work Around on One Needle, Sarah Hauschka's Magical "Unvention"*. Fiber Trends, 2002.

Gibson-Roberts, Priscilla. *Simple Socks: Plain and Fancy*. Nomad Press, 2004.

Gillingham, Antje. *Knitting Circles Around Socks: Knit Two at a Time on Circular Needles*. Martingale and Company, 2007.

Morgan-Oakes, Melissa. *2-at-a-time Socks: Revealed Inside...The Secret of Knitting Two at Once on One Circular Needle Works for any Sock Pattern!* Storey Publishing, 2007.

Websites

Google
http://www.google.com

Knitter's Review
http://www.knittersreview.com

Knitty
http://www.knitty.com

Persistent Illusion
(Judy Becker's website)
http://www.persistentillusion.com

Ravelry
http://www.ravelry.com

Sock Knitter's List
http://www.socknitters.com

This book's website
http://www.toeupsockbook.com

You Tube
http://www.youtube.com

Index

Photo Key

This key lists all photos not specifically identified with a pattern so that, if you see a sock you just have to make, you can easily identify which pattern it goes with.

Front Cover - *Sakura*, p. 123
Table of Contents, bottom - *Mix-and-Match Rib Sock Recipe*, p. 62
Montage on p. 9, upper - *Gull Wing*, p. 76
       lower left - *Old-School Knee-Highs*, p. 70
       lower right - *Syncopated Rib Boot Socks*, p. 67
Gauge and Fabric for Socks on p. 18 - *Sakura*, p. 123
Color on p. 19 - *Gull Wing*, p. 76
Non-Shaped Round Toe on p. 30 - *Mix-and-Match Rib Sock Recipe* (Baby Cable Rib), p. 62
Shaped Round Toe on p. 31 - *Vortex*, p. 100
Anatomical Toe on p. 32 - *Syncopated Rib Boot Socks*, p. 67
Star Toe on p. 33 - *Fjordland*, p. 83
Short-Row Toe on p. 34 - *Peace Lily*, p. 117
Short-Row Heel on p. 37 - *Mix-and-Match Rib Sock Recipe* (Baby Cable Rib), p. 62
Hybrid Heel on p. 39 - *Vortex*, p. 100
Afterthought Heel on p. 40 - *Syncopated Rib Boot Socks*, p. 67
Star Heel on p. 42 - *Old-School Knee-Highs*, p. 70
Yarn Over Bind-Off on p. 43 - *Mix-and-Match Rib Sock Recipe* (Baby Cable Rib), p. 62
Sewn Bind-Off on p. 45 - *Fjordland*, p. 83
P2tog Bind-Off on p. 46 - *Mix-and-Match Rib Sock Recipe* (Bamboo Rib), p. 62
Caring For Your Socks on p. 48 - *Peace Lily*, p. 117
Montage on p. 56, upper left - *Spring in Oregon*, p. 109
       upper right, top - *Mix-and-Match Rib Sock Recipe*, p. 62
       upper right, center - *Candelabra*, p. 96
       upper right, bottom - *Fjordland*, p. 83
       lower - *Old-School Knee-Highs*, p. 70